SWEATERS FROM
A NEW ENGLAND VILLAGE

20 Original Patterns Featuring Harrisville Designs Yarn

SWEATERS
from a
NEW ENGLAND VILLAGE

By Candace Eisner Strick

Down East Books / Camden, Maine

COPYRIGHT © 1996 BY CANDACE EISNER STRICK
PHOTOGRAPHS ON PAGES 7–9 USED BY PERMISSION OF HISTORIC HARRISVILLE, INC.
PHOTOGRAPHS ON COVER AND PAGES 11–26 BY LYNN KARLIN
ISBN 0-89272-358-0
LIBRARY OF CONGRESS CATALOG CARD NUMBER: 95-72159
COLOR SEPARATIONS BY HIGH RESOLUTION, CAMDEN, ME.
PRINTED AND BOUND AT BOOKCRAFTERS, INC., FREDERICKSBURG, VA.

2   4   5   3

DOWN EAST BOOKS, P.O. BOX 679, CAMDEN, MAINE 04843

CONTENTS

In loving memory of my mother, Sarah Greenspan Eisner,
who taught me to knit.

To my father, Raymond H. Eisner,
whose skill, creativity, and artistry never cease to amaze me;
and to my husband and life's partner, Kenneth L. Strick,
for his support, patience, and abiding love.

INTRODUCTION

My purpose in writing this book is to introduce knitters to the beauty of Harrisville Designs' yarns. Tucked away in the peaceful hills of New Hampshire, Harrisville offers the most extensive color line of almost any company that I know of. The colors were an inspiration to me, and when I started putting them together with designs, there was no end to the possibilities.

When I first discovered Harrisville I was interested only in the yarns. However, I soon discovered that there was a whole interesting and unique history to this little village, one that made the yarn all the more special. I have included a brief history of the mills at Harrisville. It's fascinating to see how today's business builds on the two-hundred-year traditions of this New England settlement.

I have assumed that the knitters who use this book know most of the basic techniques. However, there are a few specialized techniques that I explain in detail, such as steeking. I hope to conquer the reluctance of many knitters to use this wonderful process by carefully explaining it step-by-step. Steeking is described in each pattern where it is used and is also explained thoroughly in the "Tips and Techniques" chapter.

I have always been angered by knitting charts that show no lines of increase or decrease, and instructions that simply say, "Keeping continuity of pattern. . . ." Therefore, all the charts in this book clearly show every stitch in the pattern. There is no need for the knitter to reproduce extra charts or to draw in lines.

There are patterns ranging from one-color textured designs to Fair Isle designs calling for ten or more colors. Yarn weights range from thick worsted to Shetland weight; techniques from straight knitting, to circular, to combinations of both. I hope that knitters will find these designs both rewarding and satisfying to make, and that a whole new world of inspiration will be introduced to you from a tiny village in New Hampshire.

ACKNOWLEDGMENTS

Many people have inspired and helped me along the way, from the very beginnings of my love of knitting to the final draft of this book. My wonderful friend Felicity Harley was the first to encourage me to become a knitwear designer, and she also helped me draft my very first letter to Harrisville Designs. Thank you to Dody and Doty Knight, for introducing me to Harrisville and for a warm friendship that has encompassed everything from violin bows to Shaker cheese baskets; to Patrick McGlamery for showing me his Fair Isle vest, and to Carrie Crompton for her sound advice. My very talented fiber artist friend Dahlia Rechel gave me the opportunity to play with colors and fibers while weaving. With her help and guidance, my sense of color began to evolve.

Thank you to my sisters Judith and Ardeth, who have been broadcasting the coming of this book throughout Minneapolis–St. Paul and the greater Boston area, and to all of my knitting friends who have given me encouragement and praise throughout the writing of this book. At Harrisville Designs, special thanks go to owners John and Pat Colony and Jennie Wood, director, who have made my dream come true and helped with this project in every possible way. And thanks to Karin Womer, editor, and Thomas Fernald, publisher, at Down East Books, for having faith in me.

My entire family deserves a huge thank you for living through two years of "knitting obsession." Thanks to my three sons—Nathaniel, Liam, and Noah—for telling people that their mother sits around all day and knits, and to my parrot, Vincent van Gogh (affectionately called Go-Go), who bites all my stitch markers in half but has kept me company through billions of stitches. More than thanks go to my husband, Ken, for gently hurling me into the twentieth century by trying to teach me the mysteries of our computer. His patience, sense of humor, and encouragement have prevented the computer from being hurled, not gently, through the window by the fiber artist, whose technology lies in the eighteenth century. It was a rare coincidence indeed that I should fall in love with a man whose last name means "knit" in German.

SOURCES

The yoke motif of the Sea Mist Gansey is from Elvira Parlini-Ruffini, *Charted Swiss Folk Designs,* rendered by Hanna Reinholte (New York: Dover Publications, Inc., 1978).

The Little Birds cable design is from Barbara G. Walker, *A Treasury of Knitting Patterns* (New York: Charles Scribner's Sons, 1968).

The Norwegian Sweater braid comes from Lizbeth Upitis, *Latvian Mittens: Traditional Designs and Techniques* (St. Paul: Dos Tejedoras, 1981).

Background information about the town of Harrisville and its mills came from the following sources.

• John Borden Armstrong, *Factory Under the Elms: A History of Harrisville, New Hampshire 1774–1969,* published for the Merrimack Valley Textile Museum (Cambridge, Mass.: M.I.T. Press, 1985).

• Mary Meath, *The Warp and Weft of a Textile Village,* pamphlet (Harrisville, N.H.: Historic Harrisville, Inc., 1985).

• William Pierson, "Harrisville, New Hampshire" *Antiques Magazine* (October 1972).

• "A Dead Mill Town Returns to Life," *New England Business Magazine* (August 16, 1979).

Other publications referred to in the text are:

• Sue Bender, *Plain and Simple: A Woman's Journey to the Amish* (New York: HarperCollins Publishers, 1989).

• Jeanne DuPrau, *The Earth House* (New York: Fawcett Columbine, 1992).

• Alice Starmore, *Alice Starmore's Book of Fair Isle Knitting* (Newtown, Conn.: Taunton Press, 1988).

▦ WHY KNIT?

The wonderful selection of colors in the Harrisville yarns makes them a natural choice for use in Fair Isle sweaters. They are also available in the fine weights traditionally used for Fair Isle. Thirteen of the designs in this book are in the Fair Isle style and appear, at first glance, to be very intricate. Many knitters instantly decide against making a Fair Isle sweater as soon as they hear that it is knit with many colors and on small needles. If the idea of steeking and cutting is thrown in at the same time, they become even more closed-minded. This is unfortunate because following a charted design and working with only two colors in a row is actually an easily learned technique, one that becomes quite automatic after a while. It yields startlingly beautiful results for such a small amount of effort.

If one knits a sweater purely for utilitarian reasons, then a one-color, plain sweater fits the bill. However, in our day and age, we rarely knit a sweater just to keep someone warm. Knitting is as much a pleasurable hobby as it is a practical one. The process gives us enjoyment, and at the same time yields a useful and beautiful end result. Sue Bender expressed it well in her book *Plain and Simple: A Woman's Journey to the Amish*: "It is the enjoyment of every step in the process of doing; everything, not only the isolated piece we label art. If accomplishing is the only goal, all that it takes to reach that goal is too slow, too fatiguing—an obstacle to what you want to achieve. If you want to rush to the accomplishment, it is an inevitable disappointment. Then you rush to something else. The disappointment is reaped over and over again. But if every step is pleasant, then the accomplishment becomes even more, because it is nourished by what it going on."

For those knitters who dread working on small needles, I encourage you to try it. Small needles are much more comfortable to work with, and they produce a subtle, sophisticated fabric. The fineness of the yarn, doubled in thickness due to the carried colors, produces a lightweight, warm sweater. It just takes a little more time. "Making a beautiful thing takes time, attention, and care," writes Jeanne DuPrau in *The Earth House*.

Knitting is not something that requires a huge block of uninterrupted time. It can be picked up at odd intervals and worked on a little bit at a time. It is portable, lightweight, and eminently satisfying. There is no such thing as wasted time when you have your knitting with you. It can turn an otherwise nightmarish wait in a doctor's waiting room to a pleasurable interlude. The colors and designs of what I am knitting fascinate and inspire me as I watch the design unfold itself row after row. I believe that everyone needs some sort of visual beauty everyday in their lives, whether it is a wonderful painting, a gorgeous landscape, a walk in the woods, or a beautiful piece of fabric or quilt. My knitting and yarns are always within my sight, and so I remain visually satisfied. The repetitive motions of creating the stitches are relaxing, rhythmic, and sometimes hypnotic.

Knitting while walking takes the rhythm one step further. A small project such as socks or mittens is the perfect thing to do while on a walk. Tuck the ball of yarn into a pocket or wear a waistbelt. You may have to start out doing both a bit slower than usual, but with practice, you will even be able to look up once in a while to wave to the people who stare at you from cars. Weather permitting, this is one of my favorite pastimes, combining two of the things that I love to do into one activity.

If nothing else, being a knitter at least provides an excuse to buy fiber. My philosophy on this is very simple: If you like it, buy it. You can never have too much yarn. In order to have inspiration, you must have enough variety to choose from. And inspiration sometimes comes at the oddest moments, often when it is not possible to go to your favorite yarn store. If you are lucky enough to be planning a new house, be sure to include a very large yarn closet with sliding doors. If you are making do with what you have, build shelves to store your yarn. Having it in full view is very important. I like to practice my cello in my "yarn room," staring at my skeins while I am playing. Some of my favorite color schemes have come about this way.

My final bit of advice is about substituting colors. Color is purely subjective. It is an individual preference, and there is no such thing as the "right" color combination. If you like it, it is right. If you want to try making one of my designs using different colors, please do. My only caution is: Be sure to knit a swatch first. Sometimes what looks perfect together in skeins does not work in the knitted swatch.

Colors that are close to each other sometimes get lost in a pattern. Conversely, colors of high contrast sometimes give a strobe effect when worked up in a pattern. If you are pleased with the result of the swatch, go for it. I wish you every success.

DISCOVERING HARRISVILLE DESIGNS

My discovery of Harrisville Designs and their yarns dates back eight years, but my love affair with yarn and knitting goes back to as long as I can remember. My mother taught me how to knit when I was three years old. My first skein of yarn was a Red Heart pull skein of rainbow variegated acrylic, and the needles were size 10 white plastic. My first attempt came out triangular due to the number of stitches that I dropped, but I was undaunted. I had discovered a passion that was to follow me through life.

Shortly after my first attempt, my mother decided that my two older sisters should be knitting themselves sweaters. Her motives were probably to keep them busy, but also, in those days, one could knit or sew a garment for much less than it cost to purchase a finished item. My mother, always frugal, probably had that in mind as we headed out to buy the yarn. Ardeth got lavender and Judith chose salmon. The yarn was acrylic, but in those days it did not matter to me. It was beautiful, pure and simple, and I was terribly jealous and angry that I was not allowed to get yarn also. Well, the sweaters dragged on and on. Ardeth finally did finish hers, although I never do recall her wearing it. Judith never finished hers, and to this day, we still laugh about the half-done pieces with holes in them!

So you might say that this was the beginning of my passion for knitting. I've learned much about yarn along the way. As a child, I looked forward to visits to the basement of Neisner's Five and Ten (our favorite store since it was our last name with an N) in downtown Springfield, Massachusetts; now I plan odysseys to an old brick building in Harrisville, New Hampshire, to buy my yarns.

My introduction to Harrisville Designs was serendipitous. My best friend, Dody, moved to the town of Nelson, New Hampshire, which is just a stone's throw from Harrisville. She discovered the treasury of beautiful yarns there and passed the word along to me.

Dody and I used to live two miles away from each other in Hebron, Connecticut, and we were both obsessed with knitting. About an hour's drive from Hebron was a Brunswick factory outlet store where the bargains were positively outrageous. We used to pile all the kids (each of us had three) into my van and drive there for the morning to pore over the yarns and patterns. We would stagger out of there with boxes of yarn that we had bought for next to nothing. Almost every morning at nine, Dody would call me with a question about something she was working on, and it was the perfect excuse to get together for coffee and knitting. Between knitting for the kids, ourselves, and husbands, we reproduced a ton of patterns!

After several hundred sweaters, Dody's husband was offered a job in New Hampshire. There went my best knitting buddy. Shortly after that, the Brunswick outlet closed. These were two devastating events in my life, but ones which were to shape the events of things to come.

Dody moved to the village of Nelson and lived in a picture perfect 1760 colonial. Going to visit was like spending a week in Sturbridge Village, but with all the modern conveniences. For Dody and me, the first part of any visit was the trip to Harrisville. The husbands were left for a few hours with the six kids while Dody and I went on our pilgrimage. The ride was down a winding dirt road, then around Harrisville lake. In the winter it was particularly scary, since there are no guard rails where the road flanks a sharp precipice. Dody never seemed to mind taking those turns at a good clip. I'd be scared, but getting to Harrisville was all I'd care about at the moment.

We would finally walk through those doors into yarn heaven. Just the smell of all that wool was feast enough, but to gaze at cubby after cubby of the most beautiful palette of colors that I had ever seen was totally overwhelming. Never before had I seen such a wide and subtle range of colors, from the most sophisticated classics to the brightest of brights, and all the shades between. From the first glimpse, I wanted it all.

Until I discovered this resource, I could only be inspired by the patterns that I had chosen to reproduce; now I was inspired by color. Any pattern could become a masterpiece in luscious color. Each trip to Harrisville made me more and more daring, and between trips there was always the option of mail order. With a color card at home there was no end to the time I could spend poring over colors and combinations. One thing lead to another, and I started designing my own patterns.

My fascination with color naturally led me to Fair Isle Designs. When my friend Patrick made a Fair Isle vest using Alice Starmore's book as his guide, I was entranced. Then he started explaining about steeking and cutting, and like everyone else who hears of cutting, I was horrified!! But his vest was a totally new experience of colors and patterns, and I went home saying, "I can do that."

With Harrisville yarns as my palette, Alice Starmore as my guide, and Patrick as moral support, I was able to design and knit a gorgeous Fair Isle sweater. Never had I felt such accomplishment upon completing a sweater. This was my first original, and, for me, the beginning of a whole new concept in knitting.

THE MILL TOWN

Harrisville, New Hampshire, is what people think of as a quaint, pristine New England village—postcard material. It is indeed a beautiful little town. But what is unique about this little town is that woolen yarn is still being spun here, as it has been for two hundred years. An average of ten thousand pounds a month of exquisite yarn is produced here. Historians appreciate Harrisville for its intact architecture and rich history; fiber artists treasure it for its yarn.

New England is home to many mill towns. Most of the old mills are now defunct, empty monuments of a once thriving industry that is now nearly forgotten. During the early part of the nineteenth century, however, these mills were the livelihood of the people who lived in the towns built around them. Unlike other New England villages where the church dominated the central location, in towns such as Harrisville the mill had the spot of importance. The rest of the community was planned and built around it. The major factor in deciding exactly where the mill was to be built was water power.

Harrisville offers a splendid view of Mt. Monad-

Cyrus Harris and partners built this granite mill in the mid-nineteenth century. Courtesy of Historic Harrisville, Inc.

nock, but that was not why the town was situated here. It was a chain of ponds, culminating in a waterfall of over one hundred feet that attracted Abel Twitchell, a mechanic, who in 1774 built a mill here to grind grain and saw wood. Jonas Clark, Abel's son-in-law, started a fulling mill to accommodate his neighbors' need to finish their hand-loomed cloth. Another son-in-law, Bethuel Harris, also joined the business. Soon wool carding was being done at the mill also.

This was the beginning of the wool industry that was to be Harrisville's mainstay for years to come. The one vital element of the mill—water power— had to be reliable. Abel's insurance was to buy the surrounding land and control the flow from the watershed.

The mill prospered, providing a service for family and neighbors. Abel built a house close by that still stands today. It is practical and plain but has a beautiful view of the valley. The settlement that grew up around the mill site came to be known as Twitchell's Mills.

In time, Abel Twitchell and Jonas Clark went on to other things, and Bethuel Harris launched into full-time carding, fulling, and cloth production. Water-powered looms, which were introduced only ten years earlier, were added to the mill. This was 1813, and American-made goods were in demand. Bethuel and his wife, Deborah, had many children, and at least seven of them, along with in-laws, helped out in the mills. In 1830, the village became known as Harrisville. There were several mills by then, along with a prospering village.

After 1850, however, the village began to change. An additional new mill was built by Bethuel's son Cyrus and two business partners. Then, due to the untimely deaths of Cyrus Harris and one of his partners, the new stone building had to be sold. Faulkner and Colony, a woolen company from Keene, New Hampshire, took over.

The Colony family had been in Keene for three generations. They had years of experience in running woolen mills, were financially stable, and had many connections in the industry. Through the Cheshire Mills (as they named their new acquisition), they were able to double woolen production and market their products successfully.

Increased production meant that the mills needed a bigger work force. Family, neighbors, and friends were not able to fill the need anymore. Boarding houses were built to accommodate the new workers coming to the area. People of different ethnic backgrounds began living and working in the village. Technology was expanding, and the country was in the middle of the Civil War.

Always alert to new ideas, the Colonys and Harrises agreed that a railroad was the best way of bringing in raw goods and shipping out finished products. However, a railroad required subsidies from the towns it was to serve, and Dublin and Nelson, the townships where Harrisville village was located, refused to go along. Milan Harris petitioned the state legislature to lay out a new township, and on July 2, 1870, Harrisville officially became a separate town.

The mills continued to thrive, and by 1882, all the Harris mills and water rights were owned by the Colonys. By 1860, annual sales were about $200,000. By the early 1900s, the Cheshire Mills were operating with forty-four broadlooms and four thousand spindles, making it a larger than average operation. The company was big enough and stable enough to weather several recessions. Just before 1940, employment reached about two hundred and sales were $2 million.

After World War II, however, trouble set in for most New England textile mills. The South offered much lower labor costs, and eventually overseas mills undercut all domestic producers. The end of an era was near. Between the end of World War II and 1970, the United States textile industry had gone from 90,000 wool-producing broadlooms to a mere 5,000.

The mills in Harrisville limped along. But in 1970, along with 54 other mills in New England, Cheshire Mills closed its doors for good. The company, whose property included all the mill buildings, the machinery, and many houses, faced liquidation on the auction block. It was an overwhelming problem, but after years of proud history, the townspeople were not willing to give up.

Historic Harrisville, a nonprofit organization made up of local people, along with John Colony III, one of the fifth generation of that family to be involved with Harrisville, focused on the preservation of the village. Their vision included sustaining the tradition of textile production not as a working museum but as a viable wool processing business. The sale of one of the big mill facilities to a water filter manufacturer provided employment and tax base to keep the village viable, and sixty people are now employed by that company. Harrisville Designs then began manufacturing the high-quality yarn that has become their trademark. They started out using some of the equipment from the Cheshire Mills.

This brings us to the present retail showroom, which was built as the Harris storehouse in 1832. Here one finds skeins and cones of beautiful and endless colors, silently paying tribute to a long and proud history and waiting to be turned into a knitted or woven masterpiece. *(Text continues on page 10.)*

Housing was provided for some of the mill employees: a Harris tenement on Kadaket Street. Courtesy of Historic Harrisville, Inc.

McCall's Blacksmith Shop stood on Prospect Street. Courtesy of Historic Harrisville, Inc.

One mill family poses for a portrait outside their company house. Courtesy of Historic Harrisville, Inc.

This brick mill was built between 1924 and 1926. The weaving room occupied the top floor; the carding room and spinning frame room were on the lower floor. In the foreground is a rope drive built in 1890. Courtesy of Historic Harrisville, Inc.

FROM SHEEP TO SWEATER

Today, an average of twenty-five hundred pounds of yarn a week, ten thousand pounds a month, is produced in Harrisville. There are sixty-three regular colors and twenty-three tweed colors in the Harrisville line, along with twenty-two colors in the Twitchell Mills line. All of these shades are created from fifteen standard colors of dyed fleece. But it all starts with a plain white sheep.

The whiter the fleece, the brighter and more consistent the dyed colors can be. From New Zealand the Harrisville mill imports wool that is bright white, with a fine, nice crimp (the curl in the wool) and a medium staple (the length of the fibers). Because New Zealand offers a climate where the sheep can stay out on pasture year-round, the animals stay cleaner than if they were confined to a barn. The wool comes to this country already scoured, and is sent to a dyer in Philadelphia. The dyed wool is then shipped to New Hampshire in huge bales.

At Harrisville, certain proportions of colors are combined and carded (combed) together before spinning. The result is a dyed-in-the-wool yarn. The advantage of dyed-in-the-wool is that it allows for a greater range of subtle and unusual colors and produces a yarn with a heathery look. (Many other brands of yarn are carded, spun, and then dyed, which results in a uniform, flat color.) If the yarn is to have colored nubs, handfuls of the woolen confetti are thrown in while the wool is being carded. This assures that the nubs will stick during the spinning process.

After carding, the wool is rolled into thin strands of roving (at Harrisville, it's referred to as roping) that are ready to be spun. The final product of carding is a huge roll of twelve to twenty-four of these strands, ends tied together in a neat knot. If an end becomes lost, it is virtually impossible to find it.

The next step is the spinning. Each strand of roving is fed into a separate slot on the spinning machine, and twenty-four ends of yarn are simultaneously spun and wound onto bobbins. The bobbins are taken to the plying machine, where two strands of yarn are twisted together. After this, carts of bobbins filled with plied yarn are wheeled into a steamer, where a gentle steam sets the twist, much the same as steam-curling your hair. It is then wound onto cones or into skeins and labeled, ready for purchase.

(Photographs of the carding and spinning processes and the Harrisville Designs showroom appear in the color section that follows.)

VILLAGE COLORS

(Photographs by Lynn Karlin)

FIDDLEHEAD   BUTTERSCOTCH   PUMPKIN   YELLOW

The Harrisville mill spins yarns for knitters and weavers in more than 80 colors.

Black and White pullover (page 48) and Medallion Vest (page 94).

Persian Fair Isle pullover (page 98).

Trevor Merrifield, in the Child's Rainbow Stripes pullover (page 56), and Julie Nelson, in the Color Wheel sweater (page 52), at the Harrisville Children's Center.

Owl Eyes Fair Isle pullover (page 78), worn by Harrisville Designs President John Colony III.

At today's mill, dyed wool is carded (upper left) to align the fibers, then re-carded (left) to yield an even textured, continuous bat of fiber that is ready to be formed into rovings and then spun. The spun yarn is held on wooden bobbins like those shown above until it is plied into finished yarn, then wound into skeins or onto cones.

A knitter's or weaver's idea of heaven: the retail showroom at Harrisville Designs. The Purple Tweed Waistcoat hangs in front of the yarn display shelves.

Warm colors of old brick and weathered stone are integral to the historic character of Harrisville.

The Fair Isle Scroll pullover (page 109) features traditional corrugated ribbing.

The Blackberry and Lichen Tunic (page 84), modeled by Cal Deschenes, Manager of the Harrisville Designs Weaving Center.

Fair Isle in Natural Shades (page 103) is accented with traditional two-color ribbing.

Entrelac Ski Socks (page 118) are an excellent way to use up small amounts of yarn.

The Midnight Trees pullover (page 58) is worn by Harrisville millwright Phillip Trudelle.

Norwegian Pullover (page 73). Modeled by Barbara Watkins, Financial Manager for Harrisville Designs.

The Sea Mist Gansey (page 63) was inspired by traditional patterns.

The tower of the granite mill is the focal point of the center village at Harrisville.

Tweed yarns add to the textural interest of the Sweater Coat (page 37).

Amish Star Mittens (page 121) are reminiscent of traditional quilt motifs.

Rich colors define the dynamic geometric patterns of the Rhapsody in Blue pullover (page 68).

The Tri-Color Pullover (page 41) can be knit in a range of seven sizes to fit the entire family.

Left: Purple Tweed Waistcoat (page 113). Right: Fair Isle Border sweater (page 91).

The Harrisville Public Library overlooks the pond near the village center.

Smooth-finished yarns in light or medium colors are ideal for the Little Birds pullover (page 45).

❈ TIPS & TECHNIQUES

STEEKING EXPLAINED

I had been knitting for about thirty-five years before I ever heard the word *steek*. A friend tried in vain to explain it to me, but I just couldn't visualize what was supposed to be happening. Only after knitting a sweater and actually using this method did things start to make sense to me. If you still cannot visualize this process after reading my explanation, try knitting one of the sweaters that use steeking. Even if you cannot immediately grasp the concept, just follow the instructions. Once you start doing it, it will begin to make all the sense in the world. Several of the sweaters in this book are knit using steeks, and all the steps are included in those instructions. It is possible, of course, to knit those designs without steeks, but I strongly encourage you to try steeking if you have not used the technique before.

The whole purpose of steeking is to allow the knitting of a circular sweater to continue in the round past the armholes, and even across the neck opening. This has two distinct advantages. First: Since work does not have to be turned, purling is not required. (When working with two colors, a tension change often occurs between purling and knitting, resulting in an uneven or puckered fabric.) Second: Charted designs are much easier to follow when the right side of the work is always facing. When knit with steeks, the entire sweater progresses in the round, looking somewhat like a tube with funny little insets where the steeks are.

A steek is an extra section of knitted fabric that is worked across where an opening will eventually be. For example, if a sweater is being knit in the round, there comes a point at which some provision must be made for armhole openings. Work could progress from this point on single-pointed needles, working back and forth, but by using steeks, you can continue working in the round. A few stitches are put on a pin at the base of each armhole, and then ten extra stitches are cast on, bridging the gap between the front of the work and the back. These steek stitches are worked in stockinette stitch (knit every round) in alternating colors, using the same

two colors that are used in any particular round. The color sequence is alternated on the next round. This is a way of carrying the two working colors evenly across the steek, and also produces a firm fabric that will not ravel appreciably when cut.

After the sweater is completed, the steeks are cut up the middle for the armhole and neck openings. The loose ends are carefully cut away and the five-stitch width is turned back and hemmed down, producing a neat, clean edge. Sleeve stitches and neck-band stitches are then picked up around the openings, using the stitch directly adjacent to the last steek stitch.

I have seen some patterns that use steeking only up to the level of the front neck. The remaining sweater is worked back and forth, shaping the front and back neck openings in the usual manner. This method works fine for people who have consistent tension on both knit and purl, but many knitters find it just as easy to cast on a steek for both the front and back neck. Although your work will look all bunched up and won't seem to be making much sense, it will immediately transform itself into a beautifully shaped sweater once it comes off the needles and the steeks are cut.

Once you become familiar with steeking, you may want to adapt some regular patterns to this method. However, keep in mind that steeking works best with thin yarn. The thicker the yarn, the more bulk will be produced by turning and hemming the steek. Also, very slippery yarn will not work well, as it may ravel too much when cut.

The charts in this book do not show the steeks, and numbers in the directions do not include the steek stitches. Any of the sweaters that call for steeking can be knit without using this method. Follow all directions the same, but disregard the instructions for casting on and casting off the steeks. All shaping will be the same.

I hope that you will find this method efficient and rewarding, making your charted sweaters easier to knit. There is also the added bonus of having no seams to sew when you are done knitting. (Steek hems are much less trouble to sew than seams.)

Directions for Finishing a Steek

1. Using an overcast stitch, sew through the cast-on and cast-off edges of the steek. (I use the zigzag stitch on my sewing machine.)

2. Using a sharp pair of scissors, cut up the steek between stitches 5 and 6. Trim away any knots and ends left from changing colors.

3. You may pick up your sleeve or neckband stitches now and hem down the steeks later, or vice-versa.

4. When picking up stitches, make sure to use the stitch directly adjacent to the last steek stitch, going through both loops of the stitch.

5. Turn back the five steek stitches, hemming them down by hand using an overcast stitch and a strand of the most predominant color of yarn used in the sweater. It is best to go through the second or third stitch from the edge, as these are more stable than the very edge stitch. Be careful that your stitching does not show through on the right side. (While most directions for steeking call for trimming them down to a two-stitch width, I prefer the security of keeping them at five stitches, conservatively trimming back just the ragged edge.) When you have finished, work back over the stitches in the opposite direction, forming Xs.

6. Steam gently.

UNTWISTING THE PROBLEM OF TWO-COLOR KNITTING

Knitting with two colors can be a rewarding and gratifying experience. If the yarns are handled properly, the knitting will proceed efficiently and rapidly.

When more than three of four stitches of one color are used in sequence, the color not in use must be stranded across the back and caught in with the color in use. This will eliminate any long loops of loose yarn across the back. There are several methods of doing this, and all achieve the same result. I was frustrated by the method of dropping one color and picking up another, and knew there had to be a better way.

When one knits American, or English method, both colors are handled by the right hand. In order to weave in a strand of yarn, the yarns are just given a twist. At the end of a row or round, the yarns end up in a twisted cord. To eliminate this problem one can twist on one stitch, then twist in the opposite direction on the next stitch. Another way is to alternate the direction of the twist from row to row. The problem that I find with this method is that it is somewhat slow, and I cannot seem to remember which direction to twist in order to keep my yarns from tangling.

I have found that the fastest and most efficient method of knitting with two colors is to handle one yarn in the right hand with the American method, and the other color in the left hand with the Continental, or European, method. It is a good idea not to switch colors and hands, as most knitters' tension will vary from American to European. In rows of no long runs, if the right-hand yarn is consistently stranded over the left-hand yarn, then no problems should occur. I like to weave in my run when it goes over three stitches or more. Sometimes I will let it go over four stitches, depending on the pattern, but never more. In order to be able to weave in yarns without twisting or without dropping and picking up strands, four techniques must be learned. If you are not already familiar with the two-handed method, you should practice these techniques on a sample swatch. Cast on a fair number of stitches so you won't have to stop and start rows too often. Remember to carry one color in the left hand, the other in the right hand.

Photo 1.

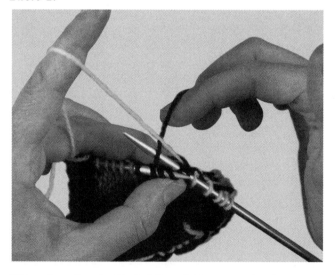

Weaving In the Left-Hand Yarn on Knit Rows. Knit three stitches with the right yarn, then, holding the left yarn a little away from the needle, bring the right yarn around the underside of the left yarn, then over the needle in the normal way.

Photo 2.

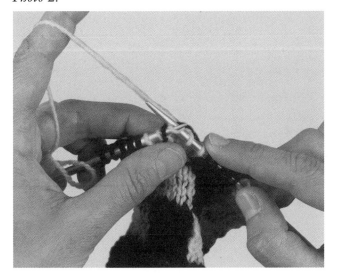

Weaving In the Right-Hand Yarn on Knit Rows. Knit three stitches using the left yarn. Insert the point of the right-hand needle into the next stitch. Holding the left yarn a little away from the needle, bring the right yarn around the back of the right-hand needle (it will be over the left yarn) and over the front of the left-hand needle. Hold it with the thumb of your left hand, knit the stitch using the left yarn, unwrap the right-hand yarn and bring it back around to the normal position.

Photo 3.

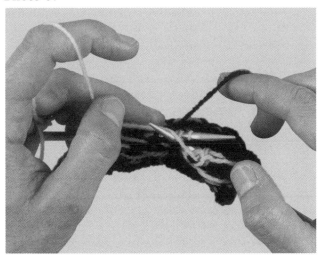

Weaving In the Left-Hand Yarn on Purl Rows. Purl three stitches using right yarn. Inset right-hand needle into next stitch. Bring left yarn over right-hand needle and purl stitch using right-hand yarn.

Photo 4.

Weaving In the Right-Hand Yarn on Purl Rows. Purl three stitches using left yarn. Insert right-hand needle into next stitch. With left yarn on bottom of right needle, bring right yarn under and around right needle and let it hang over top of left needle. Purl stitch using left yarn.

If your tension remains even and consistent, there should be no visible indication on the right side of any weaving in. However, sometimes a stitch or two of the woven-in color will show up. Should this occur, just give it a slight pull from the wrong side, and it should go back to its correct place.

When using two colors, it is easiest to use only knit stitches. This allows the front of the work to always be facing, and not mixing purl stitches with knit stitches ensures a more even tension. However, there are circumstances that call for purling with two colors. When one is proficient with these four techniques, there is no need to cringe over any patterns that call for purling or for long runs of color. Colors never need to be switched from hand to hand, and yarns never have to be dropped and picked up again and again.

CORRECTING MISTAKES

This is probably a subject that most knitters do not like to think about. We've all made that terrible, glaring mistake that, for some bizarre and unknown reason, we only notice six inches later. However, knowing shortcuts for fixing mistakes, and knowing *when* to fix them, makes a mistake a bit less painful.

When to fix a mistake: If you make a one- to two-stitch mistake under the arm, do not worry about it. If you make the same mistake in the dead center of the front, worry. There have been times when I've caught a little mistake in a very inconspicuous spot and for various reasons, such as fatigue, deadline, etc., I just left it alone. Even though I am a perfectionist, I know that no one would ever see that mistake from a galloping horse. However, if the mistake is a glaring one in a glaring place, then rip you must.

One of my funniest knitting anecdotes resulted from an incident a few years ago. My husband and I were sitting in our seats waiting for a movie to begin and we noticed a man wearing a beautiful hand-knit fisherman's sweater coming down the aisle. Ken commented on whether the sweater was hand-knit or not. He didn't think it was; I did. Eventually the man passed our row and we saw the back of the sweater. There was a huge mismatched section of design smack dab in the middle of the back!! I turned to Ken, and we both broke into hysterics. So I guess you know the moral of this story: rip it out.

How to rip: If the mistake is six inches back, then you must take all the stitches off the needles and rip. Putting the stitches back on the needles always seems to be a bit of a problem, as some of them invariably end up backward. Don't even bother about this; when you knit the next row, just knit into the *back* of those wayward stitches. This fixes them without your having to take them off the needle, turn them around, and put them back on the needle.

If you only need to rip out a few stitches, or even just one or two rows, and don't dare to take everything off the needles, you can rip out one stitch at time. You will be taking the stitches off the right-hand needle and putting them on the left-hand needle. Insert the left-hand needle into back loop of the stitch to be ripped (this is the loop that would look like a purl stitch if it were one) and slip the stitch off the right-hand needle. The correct loop will stay on the left-hand needle as the stitch.

A mistake that is just a stitch or two in the wrong color and is just a row or two back can be fixed by using the carried colors across the back as the working yarn. Slip the stitch to be fixed off the needle and undo it down past the mistake, slip it back on the needle, pick up a loop of the carried yarn in the correct color, pass the stitch over the loop. Because this may tighten up the carried yarn across the back a bit, it really only works well for one or two stitches.

The same method can also be used with a one-color, textured design. If a stitch is knit instead of purled, or vice-versa, you may make a purl stitch on the right side by doing this method from the wrong side. In a one-color sweater, this method works well for many stitches and many rows.

Swiss darning is a technique in which a stitch is actually embroidered over an existing stitch. I have never found this method satisfactory, since it makes a double thickness. However, if you absolutely missed a mistake and the sweater is entirely finished and you are beside yourself with shame, then try it. Using a blunt needle, carefully cover the stitch in question with the right color yarn. Try to form the two halves of the stitch exactly the way it would look when knit. With a lightweight yarn, the double thickness should not be too noticeable.

MAKING SIMPLE ALTERATIONS

Most of the patterns in this collection are written for at least three sizes, and, ideally, one of these sizes will fall within the range that you are looking for. There are, however, simple ways to alter some of the measurements of a pattern, such as ribbing width, sleeve length, body length, and body width. Unless you are very experienced, certain other things are best left alone, such as neck shaping and armhole shaping. The following are some suggestions for alterations.

Ribbing: Most directions call for the body ribbing to be a bit tighter than the rest of the sweater, but some people hate tight ribbing hugging their body, either because of the way it looks or the way it feels. (My friend Penny takes every new sweater of hers, wets the bottom, then stretches it over a chair to dry to eliminate that "drawn-in" look.) You can make the sweater have more of a straight silhouette by increasing the width of the ribbing to match the body. Cast on the same number of stitches as the body of the sweater, making slight adjustments for the following: if you are working corrugated ribbing or K2, P2 ribbing, your number must be a multiple of four; if you are working K1, P1 ribbing, your number must be a multiple of two. After the ribbing is completed, adjust the row of increase between the ribbing and body in order to get the right number of stitches for the body. If you want a slight bit of draw-in, just work the ribbing as written, but use the same needle size as the body. This works well, but remember to take into account that the vertical gauge also will be slightly bigger, making the ribbing a bit longer. You can eliminate a few rows if you do not want your ribbing to be longer than called for in the pattern. The same alterations can also apply to the ribbing worked around sleeve bottoms.

The above suggestions can also used to make a sweater that has a bottom other than ribbing. To convert a sweater with a ribbing to a hemmed bottom, cast on the number of stitches for the body on a needle two sizes smaller than the body. Work in stockinette stitch for about one and a half to two inches (four or five centimeters), work one row of purl on the knit side to form a ridge to turn the hem, change to the larger needle size and work the body of the sweater. To finish the hem, turn it under at the ridge row and hem stitch loosely in place.

Body Width: When writing a pattern, it is virtually impossible to take into account every type of body size. In fact, the size of some sweaters is predetermined by the design. The body width of sweaters with repeated motifs is determined by the number of stitches in each repeat. For example, a sweater with a 32-stitch repeat like the Fair Isle Scroll Sweater has to have a chest measurement of either 47.5 inches or 38 inches (120 or 96.5 centimeters). The 32-stitch repeat must be worked an even number of times in order for the motifs to be perfectly centered on the front and back and for the shoulders to match perfectly within the pattern. Therefore, to make a bigger size, one must add a total of 64 stitches, or to make a smaller size, one must subtract 64 stitches. With a gauge of 27 stitches = 4 inches (or 10 centimeters), there is an approximate difference of 9.5 inches (24 centimeters) between sizes. Patterns with stitch repeats of smaller numbers are therefore easier to alter in order to make a wider variety of sizes.

If you wish to make the body of your sweater either wider or narrower than called for in the directions, remember that you must subtract or add a total of two complete stitch repeats across front and back. You also must make alterations in the number of stitches you cast on for the ribbing, refigure the number of stitches to be worked at the round of the armhole breaks, and before the middle neck stitches are put on a holder.

Body Length: The length of the body can be altered by either adding rows or subtracting rows just after the ribbing. In a patterned sweater with a moderate-number row repeat, it is easy to add or subtract one complete repeat. With a longer repeat, however, it might be necessary to add or subtract just half of the repeat. For example, an entire repeat of 48 rows would be too long, so add just half of it, or 24 rows. With a gauge of 31 rows = 4 inches (10 centimeters), this would add about 3 inches (7.6 centimeters). Proceed with the rest of the sweater as written. Remember, you must decide before you begin the sweater whether or not you want to alter. If you knit up to the armholes and suddenly decide that you want to add half of a motif, it will throw the rest of the written charts into turmoil. Nothing will match, and you will have to rewrite the rest of the pattern.

Sleeve Length: Just as body types vary, so do arm lengths. If you wish to add length to your sleeve, add it after all shaping has been completed. In sleeves that are worked from the shoulder down, you would add extra length just before working the ribbing. Just as the sweater body begins in the midpoint of a motif, try to plan on the sleeve ending in the midpoint of a motif also. In sleeves that are worked from the wrist up, you would add extra length after all increasing has been completed and before any sleeve cap shaping begins.

Armhole Depth and Neck Shaping: I don't recommend attempting to modify these dimensions. All of my designs have fairly deep armholes and loose necks and should be ample to accommodate most body types. The sleeves have been carefully planned so that the motifs are centered at the shoulder seam and the patterns on the sleeve match perfectly with the patterns on the body when the arm is held straight down. Tampering with the armhole depth means that all these things must be refigured. To alter neck depth and width is to also refigure any borders and patterns that are to be worked around the neck opening. There is too much potential for disaster.

FINISHING & CARE OF YOUR SWEATERS

Most knitting instructions call for blocking of the finished garment. This is a method where the garment is pinned to a padded board and steam pressed to the exact measurements called for in the directions. While I have never used this method in my life, I cannot say anything against it. I have just never found it necessary to do. I generally try on my sweater before pressing. If it fits me, I just steam it lightly in order to even out my stitches and give it a more finished look. Steaming also softens the wool to some extent. If I want some part of it just a little bigger or longer, I'll gently stretch that part while steaming.

Washing Instructions: Fill the kitchen sink with tepid water and a few drops of mild dishwashing liquid. Swish the water around to distribute the detergent. Immerse your sweater in the water, very lightly swishing it around. (I avoid using the word *agitate*, as this is too violent for wool.) Let it soak for about fifteen minutes. Leaving the sweater in the sink, drain the water. Refill the sink several times with tepid water, gently swishing with each refill. When all the detergent appears to be gone, refill the sink one more time with tepid water. In a half-gallon or gallon (2- to 4-liter) container, dilute a very small amount—about two tablespoons (60 ml) of fabric softener in water of the same temperature as that in the sink. Pour into the filled sink. Swish lightly. Let the sweater sit in this for about fifteen minutes.

Drain the water from the sink. Press the sweater in the sink to remove most of the water it has absorbed. Gently lift it out of the sink in a ball and put into a towel. (Never lift it out by the shoulders, letting the weight of it hang!) Press out more of the water, changing towels each time. Spread flat to dry, gently guiding it back into desired shape. Dry out of direct sunlight and direct heat. A woolly board is helpful and can cut the drying time in half.

Washing, drying, and handling wet wool can result in catastrophe if care is not taken. A garment can shrink, felt, pill, or be damaged. The following are some basic rules for handling wet wool.

• Never use hot water. It shrinks the wool.

• Try to keep that tepid water temperature as constant as possible. Sudden changes of temperature will shock the wool and cause it to felt.

• Never lift a wet woolen garment with parts of it unsupported. The weight of the wet wool can cause damage to the shape, stitches, or seams.

• Never rub parts of a garment together or agitate in the water. This will cause shrinking and felting.

• If you are determined to spin the water out of your sweater on the spin cycle of your washing machine, do it for one minute at a time on the gentle cycle, checking after each time.

• Never use the dryer, unless you want to shrink your masterpiece to fit Barbie.

GENERAL DIRECTIONS FOR FOLLOWING THE PATTERNS

• *Read through all directions* before beginning knitting. (Note that references to charts and yarn colors are printed in capital letters whenever the directions call for *starting* a new chart or *changing* yarn color.)

• *Sizes.* Most patterns give several sizes. Instructions are given for the sizes separated by dashes (S–M–L). When only one figure is given, it applies to all sizes.

• *Measurements* given are for finished size. This is what the garment actually measures in inches. Measurements are given in inches; to convert inches to centimeters, multiply by 2.54.

• *Needle sizes* given are for American sizes. Canadian and metric equivalents are listed below. Note that sizes do not always correspond *exactly* between one measurement system and another.

AMERICAN	CANADIAN	METRIC
0	14	2
1	13	2.5
2	11	3
3	10	3
4	9	3.5
5	8	4
6	7	4.5
7	7	4.5
8	6	5

For length measurements of circular needles: 16-inch = 40-centimeter, 24-inch = 60-centimeter, and 32-inch = 80-centimeter needles.

• *Check your gauge* before beginning. Make sure you knit a large enough swatch (at least four inches, or ten centimeters, square) and measure carefully on a flat surface. A difference of even half a stitch can mean the difference of several inches over many hundred stitches. If your gauge does not correspond to the given, try adjusting needle size up or down. If the project is to be knit in the round, knit your test gauge in the round also. This can be done easily on double-pointed needles. When the test piece is finished and bound off, cut it vertically between needles 1 and 3 to yield a flat swatch.

• *Fair Isle* is a method of knitting that uses two colors in a row. Both colors are carried across the entire row. Working with two colors can produce an uneven fabric if the yarns are carried across the back too tightly. Carry all unused yarn *loosely* across the back of the work, spreading stitches on the needle to their true width. Yarns carried for more than four or five stitches should be woven in with the working yarn. This prevents large loops of yarn that could catch on your fingers when putting on or taking off the sweater.

• *Knit in any ends* left from color changes as you go along. This saves tedious darning in of ends at the completion of the sweater.

• *Intarsia* is a method of knitting that uses small sections of color. The yarn is not carried across the entire row as in Fair Isle method, but is just dropped behind the work when not in use. In order to avoid a hole at each color change, the yarns must be linked together by twisting them around each other at each color junction. Small balls of yarn can be used, but lengths of yarn are easier to handle and untangle.

• *Stockinette stitch* and *ribbing* are the cornerstones of most knitted garments. Stockinette stitch is worked differently in the round than on straight needles. When in the round, knit every round. When worked back and forth; knit one row, purl one row. Ribbing is usually worked as repeats of K1, P1 or K2, P2. Ribbing worked in only one color is generally more elastic than ribbing worked in two colors. When a variation on ribbing is to be done, directions are given at the beginning of the pattern.

• *Stitch numbers* in the directions do not include any steek stitches. The steeks are always 10 stitches wide. The numbers given refer to only stitch numbers of the actual sweater.

• The *knitted seam method* is used on almost all patterns. This makes a flat, almost invisible seam, and allows the design of a charted sweater to continue uninterrupted over the seam. This method is worked as follows.

With each set of shoulder stitches on a double-pointed needle, turn entire sweater inside out, right sides together. Hold the right front shoulder needle and the right back shoulder needle together in your left hand. Using any color of yarn that was used in the sweater, insert a third needle through the first stitch on both needles, and knit. Repeat with the next stitch, and then pass the first stitch over the second as you would normally do in a cast off. Continue in this manner of casting off until all the stitches are used. Break the yarn and pass it through the last stitch. Repeat for the other shoulder seam.

Holding the shoulders right side to right side produces a seam on the inside of the garment. Holding the shoulders wrong side to wrong side and working the seam the same way produces a ridge on the outside of the sweater. The latter method is useful if a ridge is part of the design pattern, as in Medallion Vest or Sea Mist Gansey.

• *Casting on.* There are many methods of casting on, but the one that I have found to be consistently the best is the cable edge cast-on. This produces a firm but elastic edge with no holes between the stitches. Make a loop on the left-hand needle, insert the right-hand needle through this loop from front to back, pull the loop through as if to knit but turning the loop and putting it on the left hand needle. Continue casting on, but from now on insert the right-hand needle *between* the two stitches.

• *Decreasing.* Two methods are used; one produces a decrease that slants to the left; the other slants to the right. Both methods eliminate one stitch at a time.

SSK—This method slants to the left. Slip two stitches knitwise, one at a time, to right needle, then insert point of left needle into the fronts of both these stitches and knit them together.

K2 together—This method slants to the right. Insert the right needle as usual through two stitches and knit them together.

• *Increasing.* Knit into the stitch below the next stitch, then knit the stitch as usual. This makes one new stitch.

• *Joining Rounds.* Before joining, make sure that the stitches are not twisted around the needles. It is very easy to overlook this, so check several times that all stitches are laying correctly.

• *English or American method of knitting:* The yarn is held in the right hand.

• *Continental or European method of knitting:* The yarn is held in the left hand.

READING THE CHARTS

Every square on a chart represents a stitch. Every horizontal row of squares represents a row or round. When knitting in the round, charts are always read from right to left, bottom to top. When knitting back and forth on straight needles, right-side rows are read from right to left, wrong-side rows are read from left to right; bottom to top.

On the Fair Isle designs, I have purposely not filled in background colors with symbols. I believe it makes a chart confusing to read and obscures the actual pattern. Only pattern colors are shown in symbols; background colors are designated by brackets on the edge of the chart.

Keeping your place on a chart is the crux of the issue. I have found Post-It™ notes to be most helpful. I put them directly above the current row. This shows the portion of the chart that has already been completed as well as the row that is being worked. If all work is done in relation to the last completed row, mistakes are easier to spot. The notes pull off cleanly and can be reused a number of times. I also like to use a clipboard with a sliding ruler, but this is slightly less portable. Magnetic boards also work well.

YARN

All designs in this book call for Harrisville Designs yarns. If you wish to substitute another brand, make sure that the gauge works out to what is printed. All amounts called for apply to Harrisville yarns and are based on average requirements. Since individual styles of knitting can vary, amounts should be regarded as approximate. If you plan on substituting yarn, please be aware that the number of yards contained in a specific weight can differ significantly from brand to brand.

To find the Harrisville dealer nearest to you, or for information about their yarn sample catalog, call 1-800-338-9415 or write to: Harrisville Designs, Box 806, Harrisville, NH 03450.

Because some of the designs call for only small amounts of certain colors, there will be significant amounts of some colors left over. Treasure these leftovers, as there are a myriad of things to knit and do with them, such as making the Amish Star Mittens or Entrelac Ski Socks.

THE PATTERNS

⊞ SWEATER COAT

This one-size sweater coat is warm, comfortable, and easy to knit. Pockets add practicality, and the different flecks of color in the yarn give it the look of tweed. (Pictured on page 22.)

YARN: Twitchell Mills (4 oz/113 gm skeins)

COLOR	SKEINS
A. Madder Tweed	2
B. Charcoal Tweed	6

NEEDLES: #6 and #8 single-pointed

GAUGE: 16 sts and 24 rows = 4 inches (worked in pattern on #8 needles).

FINISHED CHEST SIZE: 52.5 inches.

(For information on converting measurements and needle sizes to metric equivalents, see page 33.)

ACCESSORIES: 8 buttons (⅞-inch)

BACK: With #6 needles and COLOR A, cast on 104 sts. Work the following 2 rows of ribbing for 2 inches, ending with a wrong-side row.

Row 1: (right side) K3, *P2, K2*, repeat between *s to last 5 sts, P2, K3.

Row 2: (wrong side) P3, *K2, P2*, repeat between *s to last 5 sts, K2, P3.

Change to #8 needles and COLOR B, establishing PATTERN as follows.

Row 1: K6, P2, *K16, P2*, repeat between *s to last 6 sts, K6.

Row 2: P6, K2, *P16, K2*, repeat between *s to last 6 sts, P6.

Rows 3–16: Repeat rows 1 and 2.

Row 17: Purl.

Row 18: Knit.

Row 19: K15, P2, *K16, P2*, repeat between *s to last 15 sts, K15.

Row 20: P15, K2, *P16, K2*, repeat between *s to last 15 sts, P15.

Rows 21–34: Repeat rows 19 and 20.

Row 35: Purl.

Row 36: Knit.

Repeat these 36 rows for pattern.

Work in pattern for 102 rows.

Shape Armholes: At the beginning of rows 103 and 104, cast off 8 sts. (88 sts.) Rows 105–172: Work in pattern as established. Place 29 sts on a holder for right shoulder, 30 sts on a holder for back neck, and remaining 29 sts on a holder for left shoulder.

POCKET LININGS: (Make 2.) Using #8 needles and COLOR B, cast on 22 sts. Beginning with a knit row, work 26 rows of stockinette stitch. Place sts on a holder.

RIGHT FRONT: With #6 needles and COLOR A, cast on 54 sts. Repeat the following row of ribbing for 2 inches.

Ribbing row: K3, *P2, K2* repeat between *s to last 3 sts, P3.

Change to #8 needles and COLOR B, establishing PATTERN as follows.

Row 1: K4, P2, *K16, P2*, repeat between *s to last 12 sts, K12.

Row 2: P12, K2, *P16, K2*, repeat between *s to last 4 sts, P4.

Rows 3–16: Repeat rows 1 and 2.

Row 17: Purl.

Row 18: Knit.

Row 19: K13, P2, *K16, P2*, repeat between *s to last 3 sts, K3.

Row 20: P3, K2, *P16, K2*, repeat between *s to last 13 sts, P13.

Rows 21–34: Repeat rows 19 and 20.

Row 35: Purl.

Row 36: Knit.

Repeat these 36 rows for pattern.

Work in pattern for 28 rows.

Row 29: Make pocket as follows: Work pattern for 18 sts, slip next 22 sts onto a holder and in place of these sts work pattern across the 22 sts of pocket lining (right side of lining facing you), work remaining 14 sts.

Work even in pattern through row 103.

Shape Armhole: At the beginning of row 104, cast off 8 sts. Work even through row 148.

Shape Neck: At the beginning of row 149, cast off 6 sts. Continue working in pattern and casting off every other row at neck edge: 4 sts once, 2 sts once, and 1 st 5 times. Rows 164–172: Work even on 29 sts. Place sts on holder for shoulder.

LEFT FRONT: Cast on in COLOR A as for right front. Work ribbing row for 2 inches as follows: P3, *K2, P2*, repeat between *s to last 3 sts, K3.

Change to #8 needles and COLOR B, establishing PATTERN as follows.

Row 1: K12, P2, *K16, P2*, repeat between *s to last 4 sts, K4.

Row 2: P4, K2, *P16, K2*, repeat between *s to last 12 sts, P12.

Rows 3–16: Repeat rows 1 and 2.

Row 17: Purl.

Row 18: Knit.

Row 19: K3, P2, *K16, P2*, repeat between *s to last 13 sts, K13.

Row 20: P13, K2, *P16, K2*, repeat between *s to last 3 sts, P3.

Rows 21–34: Repeat rows 19 and 20.

Row 35: Purl.

Row 36: Knit.

Repeat these 36 rows for pattern.

Work same as right front through row 28. On row 29, make pocket as follows: work pattern for 14 sts, slip the next 22 sts onto a holder, work pattern across the 22 sts of lining, then the remaining 18 sts.

Shape armhole: At the beginning of row 103, cast off 8 sts. Work even through row 149.

Neck shaping: Work same as right front, but beginning on row 150.

POCKET FLAPS: Use #6 needles and COLOR A. With right side facing, slip the 22 sts from holder onto the left-hand needle. Work the following 2 rows of ribbing for 6 rows.

Row 1: *P2, K2*, repeat between *s to last 2 sts, end P2.

Row 2: *K2, P2*, repeat between *s to last 2 sts, end K2.

Next row: Work *YO, K2 together*, repeat between *s.

Work the 2 rows of ribbing for 7 more rows. Bind off in rib.

Sew pocket lining to inside of sweater. Fold flap over at YO row and tack lightly in place, being careful to sew through pocket top only.

SLEEVES: With #6 needles and COLOR A, cast on 42 sts. Work the following row of ribbing for 4 inches, (cuffs are worn rolled up) increasing 8 sts evenly spaced on last row. (50 sts.)

Ribbing row: K3, *P2, K2*, repeat between *s to last 3 sts, P3.

Change to #8 needles and COLOR B. Beginning with a knit row, follow CHART, increasing 1 st each side of every third row 11 times, then every fifth row 9 times. (90 sts.) Work 6 rows even. At the beginning of rows 85 and 86, cast off 8 sts. At the beginning of the next 20 rows, cast off 2 sts. Cast off remaining 34 sts.

LEFT FRONT BAND: Use #6 needles and COLOR A. With right side facing and beginning at neck edge, pick up and knit 107 sts. Repeat the following 2 rows of ribbing for 9 rows. Bind off in rib.

Row 1: (wrong side) *P2, K2*, repeat between *s to last 3 sts, P3.

Row 2: (right side) K3, *P2, K2*, repeat between *s.

RIGHT FRONT BUTTONHOLE BAND: Use #6 needles and COLOR A. With right side facing and beginning at lower edge, pick up and knit 107 sts.

Repeat the following 2 rows of ribbing for 4 rows.

Row 1: (wrong side) P3, *K2, P2*, repeat between *s.

Row 2: (right side) *K2, P2*, repeat between *s to last 3 sts, K3.

Make Buttonholes: Rib 3 sts, *cast off 3 sts, rib 11 sts*, repeat between *s 7 times, cast off 3 sts, rib last 3 sts. (Eight buttonholes made.)

Next row: Work in established rib, but cast on 3 sts over each buttonhole.

Work 3 more rows of established rib. Cast off in rib.

JOIN SHOULDERS: Use the knitted seam method.

COLLAR: Use #6 needles and color A. With right side facing and starting at center of buttonhole band, pick up and knit 38 sts to back neck holder, knit the 30 sts from back neck holder, pick up and knit 38 sts down left front, ending at middle of button band. (106 sts.) Repeat the following 2 rows of ribbing for 16 rows.

Row 1: (wrong side) *P2, K2*, repeat between *s to last 2 sts, P2.

Row 2: (right side) *K2, P2*, repeat between *s to last 2 sts, K2.

Purl one row.

Knit one row.

Bind off in purl.

FINISHING: Sew side seams. Sew sleeve seams, reversing seam for bottom 2 inches of cuff. Pin sleeve to sweater, matching underarm seam and aligning middle of sleeve cap at shoulder seam. Sew sleeves into sweater. Sew on buttons. Steam lightly.

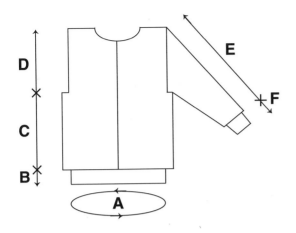

MEASUREMENTS (in inches)
- A. 52.5
- B. 2
- C. 17
- D. 12
- E. 18
- F. 2

CHART: SLEEVE SHAPING

KEY

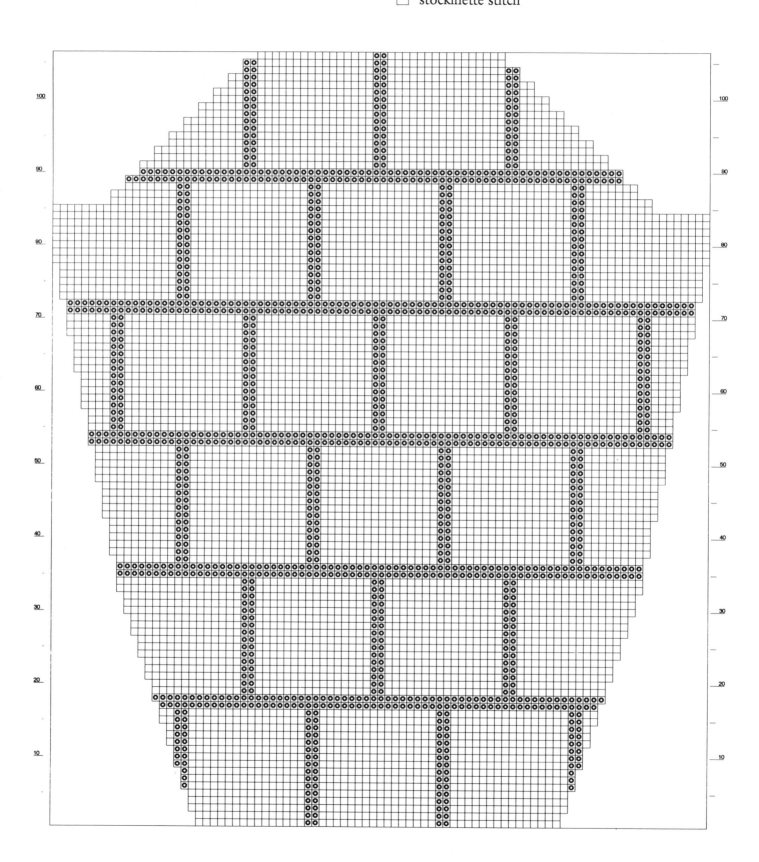

⊙ Knit on purl side; purl on knit side.

☐ stockinette stitch

TRI-COLOR PULLOVER

This easy pullover is offered in seven sizes so everyone in the family can have one. The design is made by purling on the knit rows and knitting on the purl rows. Try any three colors of Twitchell Mills yarns—they all look good. (Pictured on page 24.)

YARN: Twitchell Mills (4 oz/113 gm skeins)

COLOR	I	II	III	S	M	L	XL
A. Forest Tw.	3	3	4	4	5	5	5
B. Grape	1	1	1	1	1	1	2
C. Charcoal Tw.	1	1	2	2	2	2	2

NEEDLES: #6 and #8 single-pointed, #6 double-pointed.

GAUGE: 16 sts and 24.5 rows = 4 inches (worked on #8 needles over textured pattern).

FINISHED CHEST SIZES (in inches)

Child I	29.5
Child II	31.5
Child III	34.5
Adult Small	39.5
Adult Medium	43.5
Adult Large	47.5
Adult Extra Large	49.5

Hereafter all sizes will be referred to in directions and charts as (I–II–III) [S–M–L–XL]. When only one number is printed, it refers to all seven sizes; if in ( ), it refers to all child sizes; if in [ ], it refers to all adult sizes.

(For information on converting measurements and needle sizes to metric equivalents, see page 33.)

PATTERNS

Stockinette Stitch: K one row, P one row.

Swedish Block Pattern: Rows 1, 3, 5, and 8: P1, *K4, P2* repeat between *s to last 5 sts, K4, P1. Rows 2, 4, 6, and 7: K1, *P4, K2* repeat between *s to last 5 sts, P4, K1.

BACK: With #6 needles and COLOR A, cast on (54–58–63) [72–79–85–89] sts. Work in K1, P1 ribbing for (2) [2.5–2.5–2.75–3] inches, increasing (5–5–6) [7–8–10–10] sts evenly spaced on the last row. (59–63–69) [79–87–95–99] sts.

Change to #8 needles and CHART A. Beginning with a knit row, work between lines indicated for your size. Remember to work knit rows reading chart from right to left, and purl rows reading chart from left to right. Repeat the first 12 rows of Chart A (3–4–4) [5–5–6–7] times, then work rows 13–20. (44–56–56) [68–68–80–92] rows.

Row 21: Change to COLOR B. Work rows 21–41.

Row 42: Change to COLOR C. Work row, increasing or decreasing as follows for your size. (60–66–72) [78–90–96–102] sts.

I	Increase 1 st
II	Increase 3 sts
III	Increase 3 sts
S	Decrease 1 st
M	Increase 3 sts
L	Increase 1 st
XL	Increase 3 sts

Work the 8 rows of Swedish block pattern until Color C measures (4–5–5) [6–6–7–8] inches.

Shape Shoulders: At the beginning of the next 4 rows bind off (6–7–7) [8–10–11–12] sts. At the beginning of the next 2 rows bind off (6–6–8) [8–8–8–9] sts. Place center (24–26–28) [30–34–36–36] sts on holder for back neck.

FRONT: Work as for BACK, but when Color C measures (2.25–3–3) [3.75–3.75–4.5–5] inches, begin neck shaping.

Front Neck Shaping: Work (24–26–29) [31–36–39–41] sts, work middle (12–14–14) [16–18–18–20] sts and place on a holder for front neck. Work remaining (24–26–29) [31–36–39–41] sts. Attach another ball of yarn and work both sides at once. Decrease 1 st at each side of neck every row (3–3–4) [4–5–5–5] times, then every other row (3) [3–3–4–3] times. Work even on (18–20–22) [24–28–30–33] sts until piece measures same as Back to shoulder shaping. Bind off for shoulders as for Back.

SLEEVES: With #6 needles and COLOR A, cast on (30–34–34) [38–38–42–46] sts. Work in K1, P1 ribbing for same length as back, increasing 7 sts evenly spaced in last row. (37–41–41) [45–45–49–53] sts.

Change to #8 needles and CHART B. Beginning with a knit row, increase 1 st each side of rows

5, 10, 16, 23, and 31, then every ninth row (1–2–2) [4–4–5–6] times. (49–55–55) [63–63–69–75] sts.

Work remaining (4–7–7) [1–1–4–7] rows of Color A, ending where indicated for your size. Change to COLOR B and work the remaining 22 rows of chart. Bind off loosely in knit.

NECK: Sew shoulder seams. With #6 double-pointed needles and COLOR A, knit (24–26–28) [30–34–36–36] sts from back neck holder, pick up and knit (11–13–13) [15–15–17–21] sts down left front, knit (12–14–14) [16–18–18–20] sts from front neck holder, pick up and knit (11–13–13) [15–15–17–21] sts up right front neck. (58–66–68) [76–82–88–98] sts.

Purl one row.

Work in K1, P1 ribbing for (2.25–2.25–2.5) [2.5] inches. Bind off loosely in rib. Turn under one half of ribbing and whipstitch loosely in place.

FINISHING: Pin sleeve to body, matching center of sleeve to shoulder seam and having sleeve edges at center of body border design. Sew sleeves to body. Sew sleeve seams. Sew body side seams. Steam lightly.

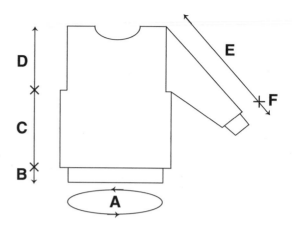

MEASUREMENTS (in inches)
A. (29.5–31.5–34.5) [39.5–43.5–47.5–49.5]
B. (2) [2.5–2.5–2.75–3]
C. (7.25–9.25–9.25) [11–11–13–15]
D. (8–9–9) [10–10–11–12]
E. (10.75–12.75–12.75) [14.75–14.75–16.5–18.5]
F. (2) [2.5–2.5–2.75–3]

KEY FOR CHARTS

⬤ Knit on purl side; purl on knit side.

☐ stockinette stitch

CHART A: FRONT & BACK

CHART B: SLEEVE

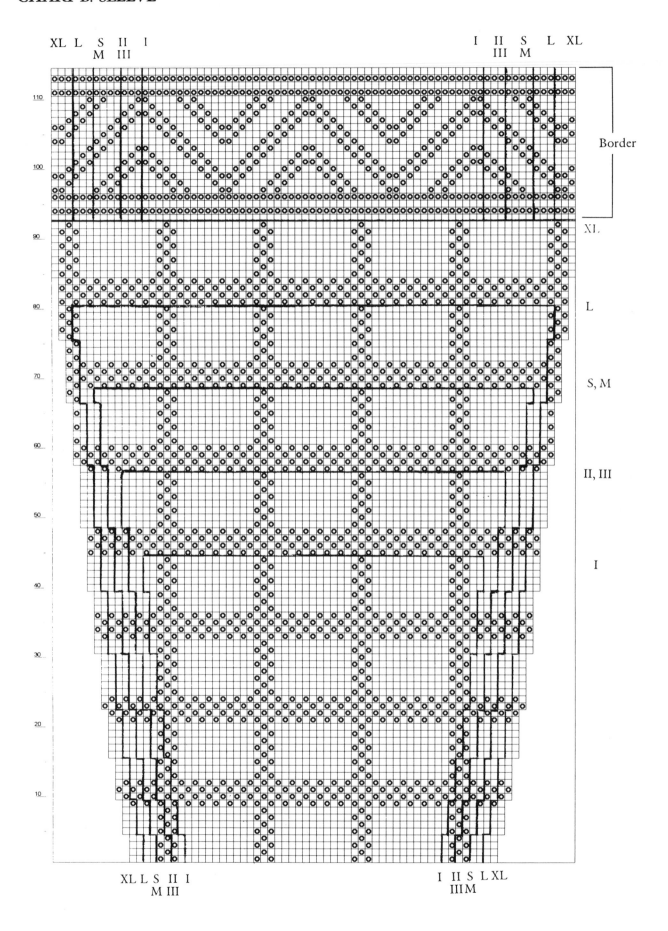

❖ LITTLE BIRDS PULLOVER

The pattern in the yoke of this sweater resembles little birds in flight. Although it uses a twisted stitch, there is no need to use a cable needle. The ribbing is also cabled by twisting a stitch. (Pictured on page 26.)

YARN: Twitchell Mills (4 oz/113 gm skeins)

COLOR	S	M	L
Cloud White	6	6	7

NEEDLES: #6 and #8 single-pointed, #6 double-pointed

GAUGE: 16 sts and 24 rows = 4 inches (worked in stockinette stitch on #8 needles).

FINISHED CHEST SIZES (in inches)

Small	42
Medium	45
Large	49

(For information on converting measurements and needle sizes to metric equivalents, see page 33.)

PATTERNS

Mock Cable: (See instructions for rows 1–4 of Back and Front.)

Stockinette Stitch: K one row, P one row.

Little Birds: (See instructions for Back, rows 15 through 23.)

SPECIAL ABBREVIATIONS

wyif = with yarn in front
wyib = with yarn in back.

BACK: With #6 single-pointed needles, cast on 71–78–85 sts. Work in mock cable, as follows, for 17–17–21 rows.

Rows 1 and 3: (wrong side) *P1, K2, P2, K2*, repeat between *s, end P1.

Row 2: *K1, P2, K2, P2* repeat between *s, end K1.

Row 4: *K1, P2, skip 1 st and knit the second st, leaving it on the needle; then knit the skipped st and slip both sts from the needle together (twist made), P2*, repeat between *s, end K1.

Repeat these 4 rows for pattern.

Change to #8 needles and beginning with a knit row, work 66–72–78 rows of stockinette stitch, in-creasing 13–12–13 sts evenly spaced on first row. (84–90–98 sts.)

Work the first 11 rows of CHART, working between the lines indicated for your size.

Row 12: Purl.

Row 13: Knit, increasing 8 sts where indicated on chart. (92–98–106 sts.)

Row 14: Purl.

Row 15: (Begin little birds pattern.) Knit 3–6–10, *slip 2 wyib, K 12* repeat between *s, end last repeat K 3–6–10.

Row 16: Purl 3–6–10, *slip 2 wyif, P 12*, repeat between *s, end last repeat P 3–6–10.

Row 17: Knit 1–4–8, *slip 2 wyib, drop next st to front of work, slip 2 sts back to left needle, pick up and K dropped st, K 2, drop next st to front, K2, pick up and K dropped st, K 8*, repeat between *s, end K 1–4–8.

Row 18: Purl.

Row 19: Knit .

Row 20: Purl.

Row 21: Knit 10–13–3, *slip 2 wyib, K 12*, re-peat between *s, end K 10–13–3.

Row 22: Purl 10–13–3, *slip 2 wyif, P 12*, re-peat between *s, end P 10–13–3.

Row 23: K 8–11–1, repeat between *s as for row 17, end K 8–11–1.

Continue working little birds pattern as estab-lished in rows 15 through 23, separating each hori-zontal set of "birds" by three rows of stockinette stitch. Work through row 65–65–69 on chart.

Shape Shoulders: Beginning on row 66–66–70, bind off 11–12–12 sts at the beginning of the next 4 rows. Bind off 10–11–12 sts at the beginning of the next 2 rows. Put the middle 28–28–34 sts on a holder for back neck.

Note: Do not start any new "birds" on the rows that will be bound off.

FRONT: With #6 needles, cast on 73–80–87 sts. Work in mock cable as follows for 17–17–21 rows.

Row 1: P2, *K2, P2, K2, P1* repeat between *s, ending last repeat with P2.

Row 2: K2, *P2, K2, P2, K1* repeat between *s, ending last repeat with K2.

Row 3: Same as row 1.

Row 4: K2, * P2, skip 1 st and knit the second st, leaving it on the needle; then knit the skipped st and slip both sts from the needle together, (twist made) P2, K1* repeat between *s, ending last repeat with K2.

Repeat these 4 rows for pattern.

Change to #8 needles, working as for back, but increasing 11–10–11 sts evenly spaced on the first row of stockinette stitch. (84–90–98 sts.) Work little birds pattern through row 53 of chart, remembering to increase 8 sts on row 13 where indicated. (92–98–106 sts.)

Shape Front Neck: On row 54, work 40–43–45 sts, work middle 12–12–16 sts and place on holder for front neck, work remaining 40–43–45 sts. Attach another ball of yarn and work both sides at the same time. Decrease 1 st at each neck edge every row 5–5–4 times, then every other row 3–3–5 times. Work 0–0–1 row even.

Shape Shoulders: Beginning on row 66–66–70, bind off for shoulders as for back.

SLEEVES: With #6 needles, cast on 36–36–43 sts. Work mock cable same as for back. Change to #8 needles. Beginning with a knit row, work in stockinette stitch, increasing 18–18–21 sts evenly spaced on first row. (54–54–64 sts.) Increase 1 st each side every seventh row 12–12–13 times. (78–78–90 sts.) Work even for 4–4–6 more rows. Work the first 11 rows of chart between sleeve lines for your size. Purl 1 row. Bind off loosely in knit.

NECK: Sew shoulder seams. Starting at right shoulder, with #6 double-pointed needles, knit the 28–28–34 sts from back neck holder (for size Large only: slip first st from back neck holder then knit remaining sts), pick up and knit 19–19–21 sts down left front, knit 12–12–16 sts from front neck holder, pick up and knit 18–18–20 sts up right front (for large only: knit the slipped st). (77–77–91 sts.) Work the following 6 rnds for your size.

Small and Medium

Rnds 1, 2, 3, 5 and 6: *K1, P2, K2, P2*, repeat between *s.

Rnd 4: *K1, P2, twist cable, P2,* repeat between *s.

Large

Rnds 1, 2, 3, 5 and 6: *P2, K1, P2, K2*, repeat between *s.

Rnd 4: *P2, K1, P2, twist cable*, repeat between *s.

Bind off loosely in pattern.

FINISHING: Sew sleeve to body, matching middle of sleeve to shoulder seam, and having edges of sleeve at middle (for sizes Small and Medium) or beginning (for Large) of zigzag pattern of body. Sew side and sleeve seams. Weave in any loose ends. Steam gently.

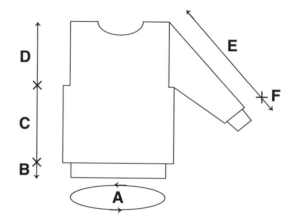

MEASUREMENTS (in inches)
A. 42–45–49
B. 2.5–2.5–3
C. 11–12–13
D. 9.75–9.75–10.5
E. 16.5–16.5–18
F. 2.5–2.5–3

KEY FOR CHARTS

☐	stockinette stitch
◔	Purl on knit side; knit on purl side
◹	slip stitch
▮	drop stitch
▯	increase
■	slipstitch for right "wing"; knit for left "wing"

CHART: BODY & SLEEVES

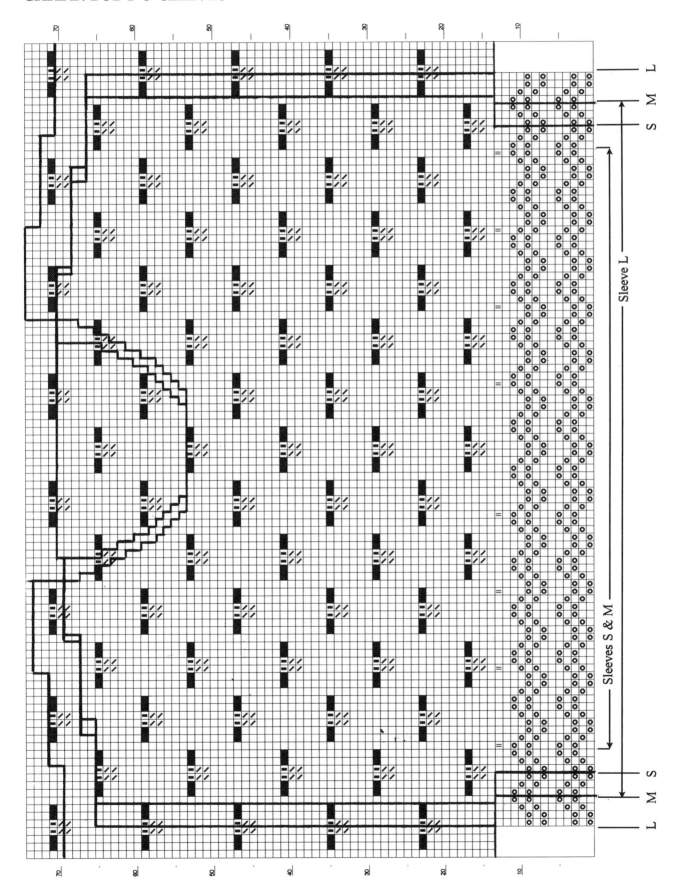

▦ BLACK & WHITE

This sweater is knit in the round up to the armholes, and then worked back and forth on straight needles. The sleeves are knit in the round from the cuff up, and then set into the armholes. Two-color cast-on and bind-off give the edges a braided effect. (Pictured on page 12.)

YARN: Harrisville Highland (3.5 oz/100 gm skeins)

COLOR	S	L
A. Black	4	5
B. White	4	5

NEEDLES: #6 circular (24-inch), #6 straight, #6 double-pointed (2 sets)

GAUGE: 22 sts and 24 rows = 4 inches (worked over pattern on #6 needles).

FINISHED CHEST SIZES: Small, 40 inches; Large, 48 inches.

(For information on converting measurements and needle sizes to metric equivalents, see page 33.)

PATTERNS

Two-Color Cast-On: With both colors, tie a knot around the needle. This is your first stitch and will be treated as a black. Cast on stitches in alternate colors but do not twist yarn; leave one color in front and the other in back. Insert needle *between* the stitches on the left needle when casting on. The side that is facing you is the right side. When joining the round, make sure that this side is still facing you.

Stockinette Stitch: When working in the round, K every round. When working back and forth, K one row, P one row.

BODY: With #6 circular needle, cast on 220–264 sts using the two-color cast-on method. Join and place a marker. Work in K1 black, P1 white for 2–2.5 inches.

Begin working from CHART A, starting on round 1–12, and working the 22-st repeat for your size 10–12 times around the body of the sweater. *Size small:* Work the 22 rounds of the chart 2 times, then rounds 1 through 20. *Size large:* Work rounds 12 through 22, then the 22 rounds of the chart 2 times, then rounds 1 through 20. (64–75 rounds.)

On round 21 of the last chart repeat, work 110–132 sts, place a marker, work to end of round This divides your work into front and back.

Divide for Armholes: On round 22 of last chart repeat, work to 4 sts before 2nd marker. Cast off next 7 sts. (Alternate colors when casting off.) Work to 4 sts before 1st marker. Cast off next 7 sts. There are 103–125 sts each for front and back. Work now progresses back and forth on straight needles. When reading chart, remember to work knit rows from right to left and purl rows from left to right.

FRONT: Using a #6 straight needle, work row 1 of CHART B, knitting 103–125 sts off the circular needle onto the straight needle. Place remaining 103–125 sts onto holder for back, or leave on circular needle. Work row 2 of Chart B (purl row).

Armhole Decreasing: Beginning on row 3, decrease 1 st at each armhole edge every other row 6 times. (91–113 sts.) Decreases are worked as follows: K2 tog at beginning of row, SSK at end of row. Remember to begin K and P rows where indicated on chart. Work to end of Chart B.

Shape Neck: Work 13 rows of CHART C. On row 14, work 35–46 sts, work the middle 21 sts and place on a holder for front neck, work the remaining 35–46 sts.

Left Front: Work 1 row. Beginning on the next row, cast off 2 sts at neck edge every other row 2 times, then decrease 1 st at neck edge every other row 6 times. Work even for 4 rows. Put remaining 25–36 sts onto holders for shoulders.

Right Front: Attach yarn at neck edge, and beginning with a knit row on row 15, bind off 2 sts at neck edge every other row 2 times, then decrease 1 st at neck edge every other row 6 times. Work 5 rows even. Put remaining 25–36 sts onto holders for shoulders.

BACK: Work CHART B as for front, then work 28 rows of CHART C. On row 29, work 29–40 sts, work middle 33 sts and place on holder for back neck, work remaining 29–40 sts.

Working each side separately, decrease 1 st at neck edge every row 4 times. Put remaining 25–36 sts on holders for shoulders.

Note: Back is worked one row less than front.

JOIN SHOULDERS: Use knitted seam method.

NECK: With #6 double-pointed needles and right side facing, beginning at right shoulder, attach both colors of yarn. Beginning with black, alternate colors when picking up stitches or knitting stitches off holders. Pick up and knit 5 sts down right back, knit the 33 sts from back neck holder, pick up and knit 5 sts up left back neck to shoulder, pick up and knit 24 sts down left front, knit the 21 sts from front neck holder, pick up and knit 24 sts up right front to shoulder seam. (112 sts.)

Work in K1 black, P1 white for 1.25 inches. Bind off loosely in knit, alternating colors.

SLEEVES: Using #6 double-pointed needles and two-color cast-on method, cast on 44–54 sts. Join and place a marker. Work in K1 black, P1 white for 2–2.5 inches, increasing 17–7 sts. evenly spaced on last row. (61 sts.) Place a marker on either side of last stitch. This last st of the round is the underarm st and is always worked in white. The increases are done on either side of this stitch as follows: Increase in first st of round, work to 1 st before marker, increase in this st, knit underarm stitch.

Begin working from CHART D, increasing 1 st at the beginning of the round and 1 st at the end of the round every third round 29 times. (119 sts.)

Work 1–11 round(s) even.

Next rnd: Bind off 4 sts at end of round (3 sts plus the underarm st).

Next rnd: Bind off 4 sts at beginning of round. (111 sts.)

Work will now progress back and forth on double-pointed needles. As the number of stitches lessen,

you can subtract a needle here and there, and when the work is about 1.5 inches from completion, single-pointed needles can be used. Remember, when working back and forth, to follow chart from right to left for knit rows, and from left to right for purl rows.

At the beginning of the next 14 rows, cast off 4 sts.

At the beginning of the next 4 rows, cast off 5 sts. Work 1 row. Cast off remaining 35 sts loosely, alternating colors.

FINISHING: Set in sleeves, matching underarm decrease line to body side, and middle of sleeve cap to shoulder seam. Weave in any loose ends.

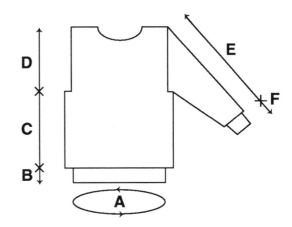

MEASUREMENTS (in inches)
  A. 40–48
  B. 2–2.5
  C. 15.75–17–75
  D. 11
  E. 19–21
  F. 2–2.5

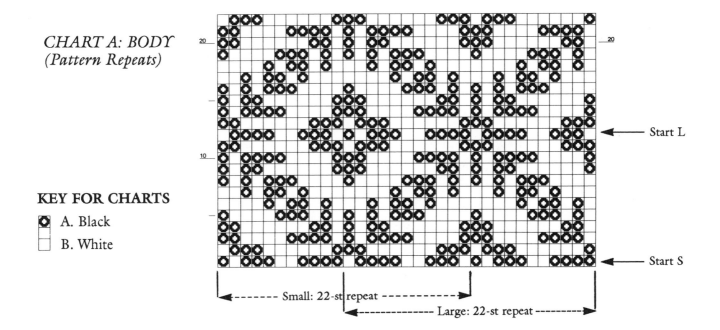

CHART A: BODY
(Pattern Repeats)

KEY FOR CHARTS
  ◉ A. Black
  ☐ B. White

CHART B: ARMHOLE SHAPING

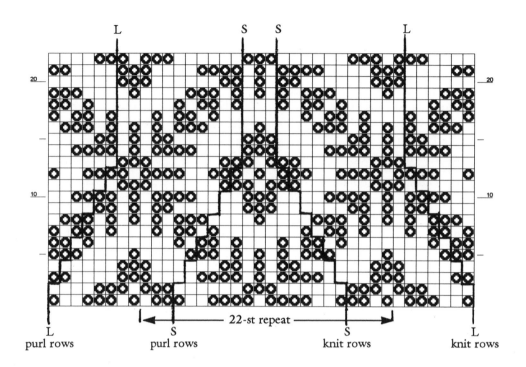

22-st repeat

L — purl rows
S — purl rows
S — knit rows
L — knit rows

CHART C: NECK SHAPING

Front is worked 1 more row than back.

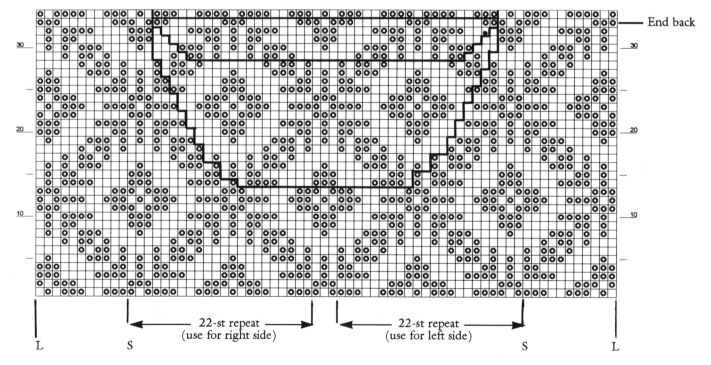

— End back

L   S   22-st repeat
(use for right side)   22-st repeat
(use for left side)   S   L

CHART D: SLEEVE

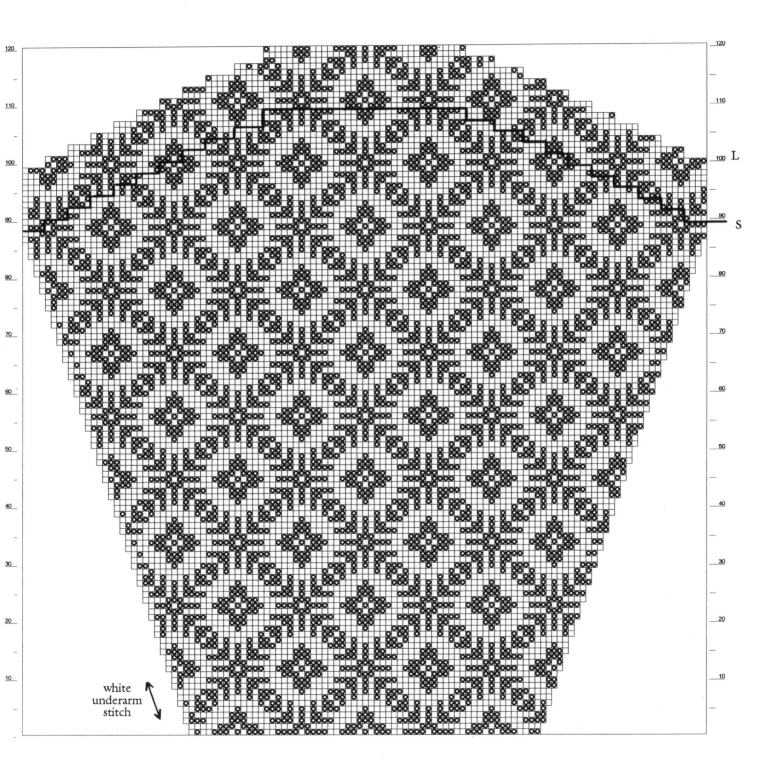

white
underarm
stitch

▦ COLOR WHEEL

This colorful sweater displays 21 gorgeous colors in the main motif. Each section of the color wheel is worked with a separate strand of yarn, using a method called intarsia. The same colors and method are used to work the diamond motif on the sleeves. Colorful blocks of ribbing complete the look. (Pictured on page 13.)

YARN: Harrisville Highland (3.5 oz/100 gm skeins) 5–5–5–6 skeins Pearl Gray (MC)

1 Color Pack, or one-half ounce of each color listed below. (For information on ordering Color Pack, see page 53.)

A. Garnet	L. Aqua Blue
B. Red	M. Bermuda
C. Topaz	N. Azure
D. Pumpkin	O. Cobalt
E. Butterscotch	P. Iris
F. Gold	Q. Cornflower
G. Daisy	R. Violet
H. Willow	S. Periwinkle
I. Hemlock	T. Plum
J. Loden Blue	U. Chianti
K. Woodsmoke	

NEEDLES: #6 and #7 single-pointed

GAUGE: 19 sts and 26 rows = 4 inches (worked over stockinette stitch on #7 needles).

FINISHED CHEST SIZES (in inches)

Small	43
Medium	44.5
Large	47
Extra Large	50.5

(For information on converting measurements and needle sizes to metric equivalents, see page 33.)

PATTERNS

Stockinette Stitch: K one row, P one row.

Twisted Rib: *K 1 in back of stitch, P 1*, repeat between *s.

Color Block Rib: Blocks of color worked in twisted rib.

Note: Colors in wheel, sleeve motif, and ribbing are worked by using separate strands of yarn for each area. Use separate balls of MC for each area. When changing colors, be sure to twist strands around each other to avoid holes. Middle circle with star motif may be worked by carrying MC and Color J across work, rather than using separate strands for each point of star.

BACK: With MC and #6 needles, cast on 92–92–102–102 sts. Work 2 rows of twisted rib. Continue working twisted rib for color block rib as follows.

Use separate lengths of yarn for each color block. *For sizes Large and Extra Large:* Rib 6 sts in Color A, 10 sts in each of the following colors: C, E, H, K, M, O, Q, R, U, then 6 sts in Color A. *For sizes Small and Medium:* Leave out the 10 sts of Color M.

Work 15 rows of color block rib. On the sixteenth row, increase 4–8–4–10 sts evenly spaced. (96–100–106–112 sts.)

Change to #7 needles and MC. Beginning with a knit row, work 53–56–73–83 rows of stockinette stitch, shaping sides by increasing 1 st each side every twentieth row, 2–3–3–4 times. (102– 106–112–120 sts.)

Begin CHART A. *Size Small only:* increase 1 st each side on row 8 of chart.

Shape Armholes: At the beginning of rows 20 and 21, cast off 4 sts. (94–98–104–112 sts.) Work through row 80.

Shape Back Neck: On row 81 work 29–31–34–36 sts, work middle 36–36–36–40 sts and place on holder for back neck, work remaining 29–31–34–36 sts. Working each side separately, work one more row. Place shoulder sts on holders.

FRONT: Work as for back through row 61–61–61–56 of Chart A.

Shape Neck: On row 62–62–62–57 work 41–43–46–50 sts, work middle 12 sts and place on holder for front neck, work remaining 41–43–46–50 sts. Working each side separately, cast off at neck edge 3 sts twice, 2 sts once, and 1 st 4–4–4–6 times. Work on 29–31–34–36 sts for 7 more rows until end of chart. Place shoulder sts on holders.

SLEEVES: *Note:* Sleeve motif is worked with a reverse of colors in certain areas for second sleeve. Work one sleeve following colors written in capital letters, then work second sleeve following colors written in ( ). Where there are no ( ), colors are worked the same for both sleeves.

With MC and #6 needles, cast on 44 sts. Work in twisted rib for 2 rows.

Work in color block rib as follows: Rib 6 sts in COLOR A, 8 sts in each of the following colors: C (U), O (T), T (O), U (C), then 6 sts in Color A. Work color block rib for 15 rows. On row 16 increase 2 sts evenly spaced. (46 sts.)

Change to #7 needles and MC. Beginning CHART B with a knit row, work stockinette stitch, increasing 1 st each side on the fourth row, then every following third row 22–22–22–18 times, then every sixth row 0–0–0–4 times, and following pattern motif from chart. (92 sts.) Work through row 86–86–86–101.

Shape Sleeve Cap: At the beginning of the next 12 rows cast off 5 sts twice, 4 sts eight times, and 10 sts twice. Cast off remaining 30 sts.

JOIN LEFT SHOULDER: Use knitted seam method.

NECK: With MC and # 6 needles, cast on 2 sts. Knit these 2 sts. They are now on the right-hand needle. With right side of sweater facing, knit the 36–36–36–40 sts from back neck holder, pick up and knit 2 sts before shoulder seam and 1 st at shoulder seam, pick up and knit 19–19–19–21 sts down left front, knit 12 sts from front neck holder, pick up and knit 19–19–19–21 sts up right front, cast on 1 st. (92–92–92–100 sts.)

Next row (wrong side): Knit, forming a ridge.

Begin color block rib. *For sizes Small, Medium, and Large:* Work twisted rib for 6 sts in Color A, 8 sts each of the following colors: C, E, F, G, I, L, N, P, R, T, then 6 sts of Color A. *For size Extra Large:* Rib 6 sts of Color A, 8 sts each of colors C, E, F, G, H, I, L, N, P, R, T, then 6 sts of Color A. Work 12 rows of color block rib, then 2 rows of twisted rib in MC. Bind off loosely in rib.

JOIN RIGHT SHOULDER: Use knitted seam method.

FINISHING: Sew neckband seam. Pin middle of sleeve cap to shoulder seam. Sew sleeves to sweater body. Sew sleeve seams and side seams. Weave in any loose ends. Steam lightly.

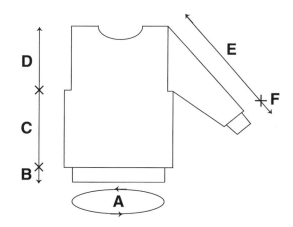

MEASUREMENTS (in inches)
A. 43–44.5–47–50.5
B. 3
C. 10–11.5–13–14.5
D. 10
E. 15.75–15.75–15.75–17.75
F. 3

CHART A: MOTIF; ARMHOLE & NECK SHAPING

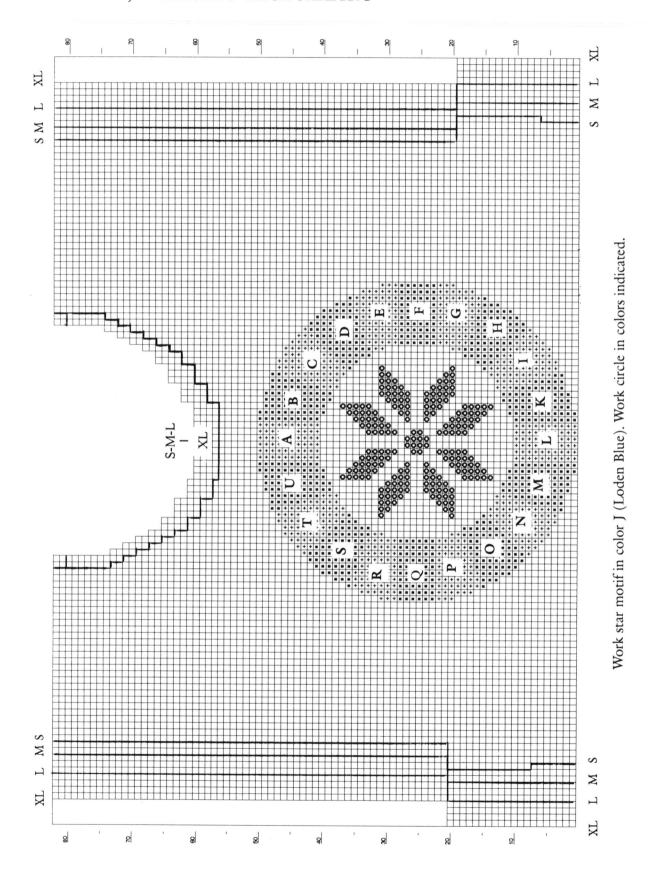

Work star motif in color J (Loden Blue). Work circle in colors indicated.

CHART B: SLEEVE

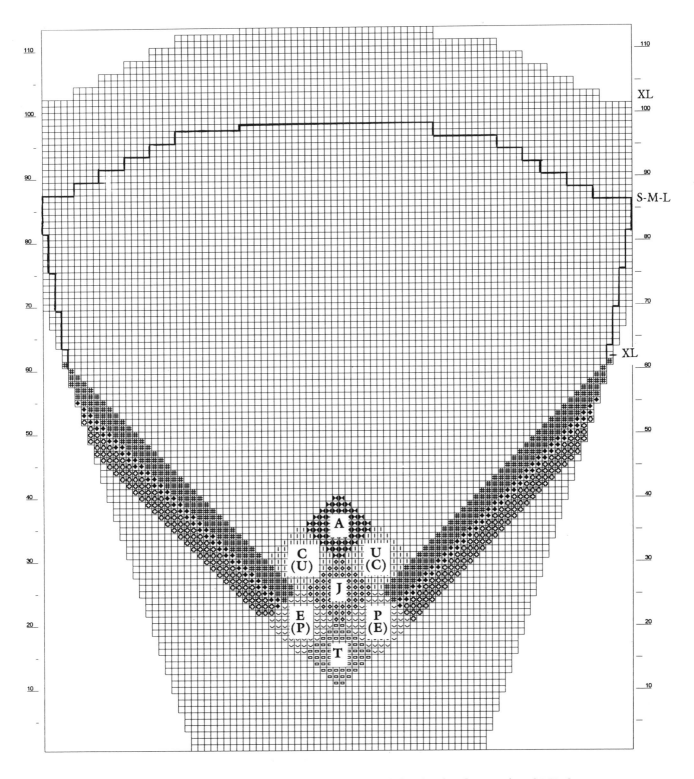

KEY FOR STRIPES

M. Bermuda

N. Azure

O. Cobalt

COLORS FOR DIAMONDS:

Sleeve #1: Use colors labeled without ( ).

Sleeve #2: Use colors labeled in ( ).

CHILD'S RAINBOW STRIPES

This sweater was designed as a companion to the adult's Color Wheel sweater. The same colors are used in the same order, but are worked in a two-row stripe sequence. Sleeves are worked in one color only. (Pictured on page 13.)

YARN: Harrisville Highland (3.5 oz/100 gm skeins) 2–2–3 skeins of Main Color (any color listed below) for sleeves and ribbing, plus 1 Color Pack, or ½ ounce of each color listed. (For information on ordering Color Pack, see page 57.)

A. Garnet	L. Aqua Blue
B. Red	M. Bermuda
C. Topaz	N. Azure
D. Pumpkin	O. Cobalt
E. Butterscotch	P. Iris
F. Gold	Q. Cornflower
G. Daisy	R. Violet
H. Willow	S. Periwinkle
I. Hemlock	T. Plum
J. Loden Blue	U. Chianti
K. Woodsmoke	

NEEDLES: #5 and #7 single-pointed, #5 double-pointed

GAUGE: 19 sts and 26 rows = 4 inches (worked on #7 needles over stockinette stitch).

FINISHED CHEST SIZES (in inches)
Small	30
Medium	33
Large	35

(For information on converting measurements and needle sizes to metric equivalents, see page 33.)

PATTERNS
Twisted Rib: *K1 in *back* of stitch, P1.* Repeat between *s.
Stockinette Stitch: K one row, P one row.
Note: Rainbow sequence is worked as 2 rows of each color, beginning with Color A and continuing in alphabetical order. When Color U is completed, the sequence begins again with Color A. Knitting in the ends from the color changes as you

go along will save tedious darning in when you are finished.

BACK: With #5 needles and MAIN COLOR, cast on 71–78–83 sts. Work in twisted rib for 2.5 inches. Change to #7 needles and COLOR A. Beginning with a knit row, work in rainbow sequence for 9–10–11 inches.

Shape Armholes: Bind off 4 sts at the beginning of the next 2 rows. (63–70–75 sts.) Work even until entire piece measures 18–19.5–21.25 inches, ending with just 1 completed row of the color you are on. Place 20–23–24 sts on holder for shoulder, middle 23–24–27 sts on holder for back neck, and remaining 20–23–24 sts on holder for other shoulder.

FRONT: Work as for back until 16–20–20 rows less than completed back.

Shape Front Neck: Work 27–30–31 sts, work middle 9–10–13 sts and place on a holder for front neck, work remaining 27–30–31 sts. Working each side separately, cast off at neck edge every other row 2 sts twice, and 1 st 3 times. Work even until piece is the exact number of rows as back. Place 20–23–24 sts on holders for shoulders.

JOIN SHOULDERS: Use knitted seam method to join front to back at shoulders.

SLEEVES: With #5 needles and MAIN COLOR, cast on 35–37–39 sts. Work in twisted rib for 2.5 inches, increasing 5–6–7 sts evenly spaced on last row. (40–43–46 sts.) Change to #7 needles and work stockinette stitch, increasing 1 st each side every fifth row 11–12–14 times. (62–67–74 sts.) Work 7–6–2 rows even.

Shape Cap: At the beginning of the next 12 rows cast off 4 sts twice, 2 sts eight times, and 6 sts twice. Cast off remaining 26–31–38 sts.

NECK: With #5 double-pointed needles and MAIN COLOR and with right side facing, knit 23–24–27 sts from back neck holder, pick up and knit 17–23–23 sts down left front, knit 9–10–13 sts from front neck holder, pick up and knit 17–23–23 sts up right front. (66–80–86 sts.)

Work in twisted rib for 9–10–11 rows. Bind off very loosely in rib.

FINISHING: Match middle of sleeve cap to shoulder seam. Sew sleeve to body. Sew sleeve seams and side seams. Weave in any loose ends. Steam lightly.

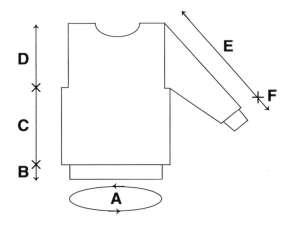

MEASUREMENTS (in inches)
- A. 30–33–35
- B. 2.5
- C. 9–10–11
- D. 6.5–7–7.75
- E. 11.5–12–13
- F. 2.5

TO ORDER THE YARN COLOR PACK

If your yarn shop does not have suitable small quantities of yarn available, you can order Color Packs from the author. Each pack contains small amounts of the 21 colors to make this sweater. *Please note:* The packs DO NOT include the skeins of Main Color specified in the directions; these must be purchased separately from a yarn shop or from Harrisville Designs (see page 34). This allows you to change the Main Color, if desired.

Send a check for $30.00 to cover materials and postage to:
Color Pack
P.O. Box 671
255 Wormwood Hill Road
Mansfield Center, CT 06250-0671

Make checks payable to Candace Eisner Strick.

◼ MIDNIGHT TREES

This sweater is worked in the round up to the armholes, then worked back and forth on straight needles; the sleeves are worked from the wrist up on double-pointed needles. The design reminds me of pine trees against a midnight sky. (Pictured on page 19.)

YARN: Harrisville Highland (3.5 oz/100 gm skeins)

COLOR	SMALL	MED.	LARGE
A. Violet	1	2	2
B. Plum	1	2	2
C. Iris	1	2	2
D. Cobalt	1	1	1
MC. Black	5	5	5

NEEDLES: #5 and #7 circular (24-inch), #7 single-pointed, #5 double-pointed (1 set), #7 double-pointed (2 sets).

GAUGE: 20.5 sts and 20 rows = 4 inches (worked over pattern on #7 needles).

FINISHED CHEST SIZES (in inches)

Small	38.5
Medium	44
Large	49

(For information on converting measurements and needle sizes to metric equivalents, see page 33.)

PATTERNS

Stockinette Stitch: When working in the round, K every row; When working back and forth, K 1 row, P 1 row.

K1, P1 ribbing.

BODY: With #5 circular needle and MAIN COL-OR (MC), cast on 158–180–202 sts. Join and place a marker. All rnds begin and end here. Work in K1, P1 ribbing in the following color/rnd sequence. (21 rnds.)

ROUNDS	COLOR(S)
3	MC
2 each	A, B, C
1 each	MC, D, MC
2 each	C, B, A
3	MC

Next rnd: With MC, knit, increasing 38–44–50 sts evenly spaced. (196–224–252 sts.)

Change to #7 needle and begin CHART A, working the 14-st repeat for your size 14–16–18 times around the body of the sweater. On rnd 67–73–79, work 98–112–126 sts, place a marker, work remaining 98–112–126 sts. This divides your work into front and back.

Divide for Armholes: On rnd 68–74–80, cast off 4 sts at beginning of rnd, work to 3 sts before next marker, cast off next 7 sts, work to 3 sts before end of rnd, cast off last 3 sts. Break yarns, pulling yarn through last st. (91–105–119 sts each for front and back. Place 91–105–119 sts on a holder for back.

FRONT: Work now progresses back and forth on straight needles. *Remember to read the chart from right to left for knit rows, and from left to right for purl rows.*

Attach yarns. Using a #7 needle, work the stitches off the circular needle for the first row. Beginning with a knit row, and starting on row 2–8–14 of CHART B (row 1–7–13 of Chart B shows the armhole divide), decrease 1 st at each armhole edge every other row 6 times. (79–93–107 sts.) Decreases are worked as follows: At beginning of row, K2 together; at end of row, SSK. Work even through row 37–43–53.

Shape Front Neck: On row 38–44–54, work 29–34–39 sts, work middle 21–25–29 sts and place on a holder for front neck, work remaining 29–34–39 sts. Working each side separately, decrease 1 st at neck edge every row 5–7–6 times, then every other row 5–4–5 times. (19–23–28 sts.) Work 0–0–1 row even. Place sts on holder for shoulders.

BACK: Work as for front through row 50–56–68.

Shape Back Neck: On row 51–57–69, work 21–25–30 sts, work middle 37–43–47 sts, and place on a holder for back neck, work remaining 21–25–30 sts. Working each side separately decrease 1 st at neck edge on the next 2 rows. Put remaining 19–23–28 sts on holders for shoulders.

JOIN SHOULDERS: Use the knitted seam method.

NECK: Starting at the right shoulder seam with the right side facing, using MC and #5 double-pointed needles, pick up and knit 3 sts down right back, knit the 37–43–47 sts from back neck holder, pick up and knit 3 sts up left back to shoulder seam, pick up and knit 16–16–18 sts down left front, knit the 21–25–29 sts from front neck holder, pick up and knit 16–16–18 sts up right front. Place a marker. (96–106–118 sts.) Work in K1, P1 rib in MC for 1 rnd, then 1 rnd each of colors A, B, C, MC, D, MC, C, B, A. Work 18 rnds of MC. Bind off loosely. Fold under and slip-stitch loosely in place.

SLEEVES: With #5 double-pointed needles and MC, cast on 39–39–44 sts. Work in K1, P1 ribbing in the same color/rnd sequence as body. Change to #7 double-pointed needles and CHART C, increasing 8–8–13 sts evenly spaced on first rnd. (47–47–57 sts.) Increase 1 st at beginning of rnd and 1 st at end of rnd every third rnd 26–26–29 times. (99–99–115 sts.) As the number of stitches increases, add extra double-pointed needles to accommodate them. Work even through rnd 80–80–93.

Shape Sleeve Cap: On rnd 81–81–94 bind off the last 4 sts of the rnd. On rnd 82–82–95 bind off the first 4 sts of the rnd. (91–91–107 sts.)

Work now progresses back and forth on double-pointed needles. As the number of stitches lessens, you can subtract a needle here and there, and when the work is about 1.5 inches from completion, single-pointed needles can be used.

At the beginning of the next 12 rows, cast off 4 sts. At the beginning of the next 2 rows, cast off 6–6–10 sts. Cast off remaining 31–31–39 sts.

FINISHING: Set in sleeves, matching underarm decrease line to body side, and middle of sleeve cap to shoulder seam. Weave in any loose ends.

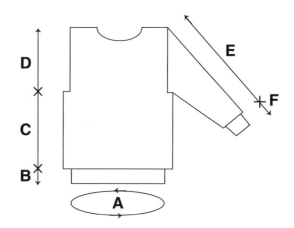

MEASUREMENTS (in inches)
- A. 38.5–44–49
- B. 3.5
- C. 12.25–13.25–14.5
- D. 9.5–9.5–11
- E. 17.25–17.25–19.5
- F. 3.5

CHART A: BODY
(Pattern Repeats)

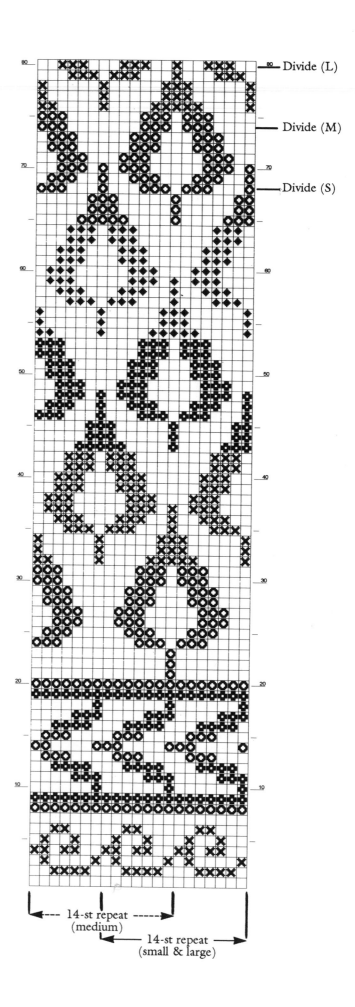

Divide (L)

Divide (M)

Divide (S)

KEY FOR CHARTS

◉ A. Violet
✕ B. Plum
✦ C. Iris
◆ D. Cobalt
☐ MC. main color

◄--- 14-st repeat -----►
(medium)

◄------ 14-st repeat ------►
(small & large)

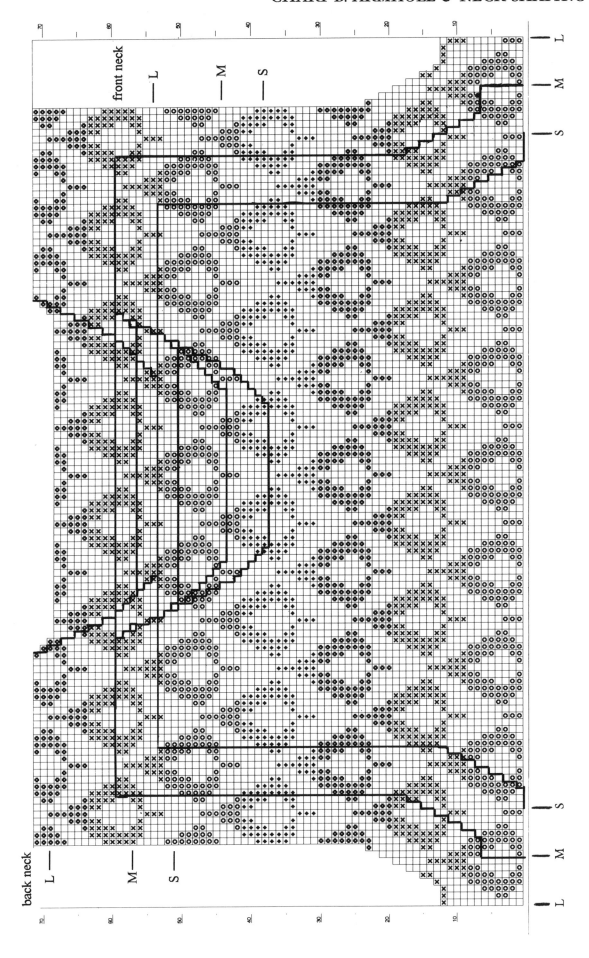

CHART C: SLEEVE

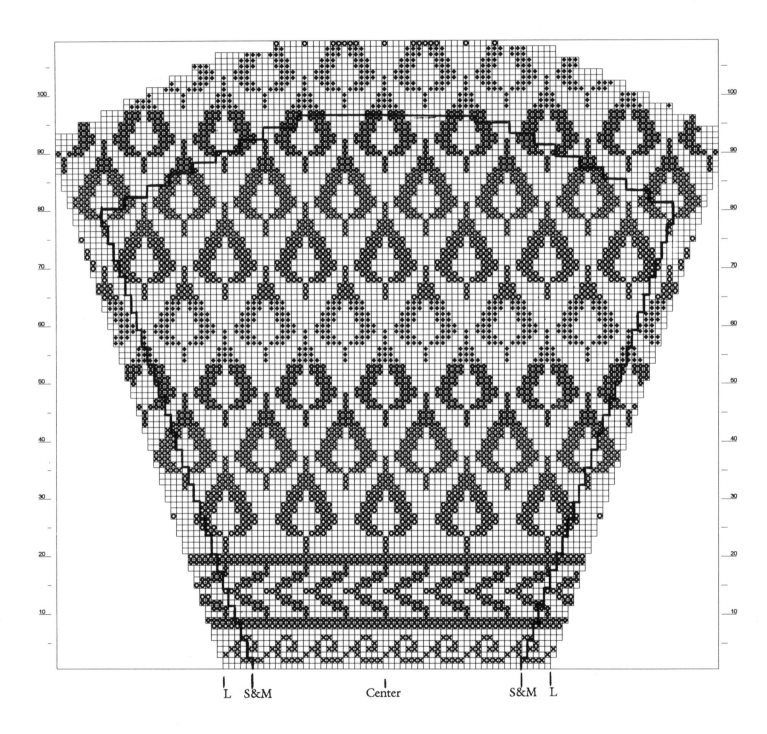

◧ SEA MIST GANSEY

Although I do not live right near the ocean, it holds a definite fascination for me. I adore the rich history and tradition of the fisherman and gansey sweaters, as well as the sweaters themselves. This gansey deviates a little from the traditional by using a large motif on the yoke and an unusual style of ribbing. It is knit in the round up to the armholes, then worked back and forth on straight needles. The sleeves are worked from the wrists up and then set in. (Pictured on page 21.)

YARN: Harrisville Highland (3.5 oz/100 gm skeins) 6–7–7 skeins Sea Mist.

NEEDLES: #5 and #7 circular (24-inch), #5 and #7 double-pointed.

GAUGE: 18 sts and 26 rows = 4 inches (worked over design on #7 needles).

FINISHED CHEST SIZES (in inches)
Small	40
Medium	43
Large	45.5

(For information on converting measurements and needle sizes to metric equivalents, see page 33.)

PATTERNS

Eight-Stitch Plait
Row 1 and all odd rows: Purl.
Row 2: K2, C4B, K2.
Row 4: C4B, K4.
Row 6: K2, C4F, K2.
Row 8: K4, C4F.

Zigzag Rib
Rnds 1 and 2: *K2, P2*, repeat between *s.
Rnd 3: *K1, LTb, P1*, repeat between *s.
Rnd 4: *K1, P1*, repeat between *s.
Rnd 5: *K1, P1, LTb*, repeat between *s.
Rnd 6: K1, *P2, K2*, repeat between *s, end P2, K1.
Rnd 7: *K1, P1, RT*, repeat between *s.
Rnd 8: *K1, P1*, repeat between *s.
Rnd 9: *K1, RT, P1*, repeat between *s.
Rnd 10: *K2, P2*, repeat between *s.
Rnds 11–18: repeat rnds 3–10.

Garter Stitch: When working back and forth on straight needles, knit every row.

SPECIAL ABBREVIATIONS

C4B or *C4F* = Cable 4 back or cable 4 front. Slip next 2 sts onto cable needle and hold at back (B) or front (F) of work, knit next 2 sts from left-hand needle, then knit sts from cable needle

LTb = Left twist back. Skip 1 st and knit into back of next st, then knit into back of skipped st. Slip both sts from needle together.

RT = Right twist. K2 together, leaving sts on needle; insert right hand needle between sts just knit and knit first st again. Slip both sts from needle together.

BODY: With #5 circular needle, cast on 168–180–192 sts. Place a marker and join. All rnds begin and end at this marker. Work in zigzag rib for 2.25–2.5–3 inches. Change to #7 needle and knit 1 rnd, increasing 12 sts evenly spaced. (180–192–204 sts.) Following CHART A, work the 6-st repeat 30–32–34 times around body of sweater. Work the 10 rnds of Chart A 6–7–8 times, then work rnds 1–9, dividing for front and back on rnd 9 as follows: Work 90–96–102 sts, place a marker, work remaining 90–96–102 sts.

Next rnd: Knit. *For size large only:* K2 together at beginning of rnd, work to 2 sts before next marker, SSK, slip marker, K2 together, work to 2 sts before next marker, SSK. (90–96–100 sts each for front and back.)

Work rnds 1–19 of CHART B or C for your size, beginning on stitch number 6–1–1 of chart.

DIVIDE FOR ARMHOLES: On rnd 20 of Chart B or C, work to 4 sts before end of rnd; cast off the last 4 sts. On rnd 21, cast off the first 3 sts of rnd, work to 4 sts before next marker, cast off next 7 sts; work to end of rnd. (83–89–93 sts each for front and back.)

FRONT YOKE: Using a #7 straight needle, work the sts off the circular needle, leaving the back sts on a holder or on the circular needle. Work rows 1–43 of chart D between lines indicated for your size, *but beginning and ending each row with 3 sts worked in stockinette stitch (shown at edges of chart).* Remember to work knit rows by following chart from right to left, and purl rows by following chart from left to right.

Shape Front Neck: On row 44, work 30–33–35 sts, work the middle 23 sts and place on a holder for front neck, work remaining 30–33–35 sts. Attach another ball of yarn, and, working both sides at the same time, decrease 1 st at each neck edge every other row 6 times. Work 4 rows even, then work 2 rows of garter stitch. Place 24–27–29 sts for each shoulder on a #5 double-pointed needle.

BACK YOKE: Beginning with a purl row, work rnds 1–59 of Chart D, working pattern within front neck outline (rows 46–58). On row 60, work 24–27–29 sts, work middle 35 sts and place on a holder for back neck, work remaining 24–27–29 sts. Attach another ball of yarn, and, working both sides at the same time, work row 2 rows of garter stitch. Place each set of shoulder sts on a #5 double-pointed needle.

JOIN SHOULDERS: Use the knitted seam method, but hold work wrong side to wrong side. This will join the shoulders and produce a ridge on the right side.

NECK: With right side facing, beginning at right shoulder seam and using #5 double-pointed needles, pick up and knit 4 sts down right back neck, knit the 35 sts from back neck holder, pick up and knit 4 sts up left back neck, pick up and knit 19 sts down left front, knit the 23 sts from front neck holder, pick up and knit 19 sts up right front to shoulder seam. (104 sts.) Place a marker. Work in zigzag rib for 1.5 inches. Bind off loosely in knit.

SLEEVES: With #5 double-pointed needles, cast on 40–44–44 sts. Work in zigzag rib for 2.25–2.5–3 inches. Change to #7 needles and knit one rnd, increasing 9–5–5 sts evenly spaced. (49 sts.) Mark the last stitch of the rnd by putting stitch markers on either side of it. This is the underarm stitch and is always worked in knit. (*Note:* Work underarm stitch in knit for *all* sizes, even though chart shows underarm stitches for size Large only.)

All increasing is done on either side of underarm stitch as follows: Increase in first stitch of rnd, work to 1 st before underarm st, increase in this stitch, slip marker, knit underarm st, slip marker. End of rnd.

Following Chart E and beginning on rnd 11–11–1, increase 1 st at beginning of rnd and 1 st at end of rnd every fourth rnd 20 times. (89 sts.) Work even through rnd 111.

Rnd 112: Work to 4 sts before end of rnd, cast off last 4 sts. (This includes the underarm st.)

Rnd 113: Cast off first 4 sts of rnd, work to end of rnd. (81 sts.)

Work now progresses back and forth on double-pointed needles. (It is possible to put all your stitches on a single pointed needle somewhere around row 118.)

At the beginning of the next 12 rows bind off 4 sts. At the beginning of the next 2 rows bind off 10 sts. Bind off remaining 13 sts.

FINISHING: Matching top of sleeve cap to shoulder seam and underarm "seam" of sleeve to side of body, sew in sleeves.

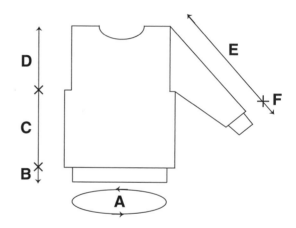

MEASUREMENTS (in inches)
- A. 40–43–45.5
- B. 2.25–2.5–3
- C. 11–12.5–14
- D. 10
- E. 18–18–19.5
- F. 2.25–2.5–3

CHART A: BODY
(Pattern Repeat)

KEY FOR CHARTS

☐	stockinette stitch
⊙	knit on purl side; purl on knit side
▨	garter stitch
I	cable 4 back
✛	cable 4 front

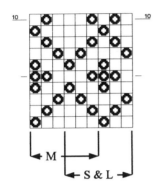

CHART B: BORDER (Medium)

CHART C: BORDER (Small and Large)

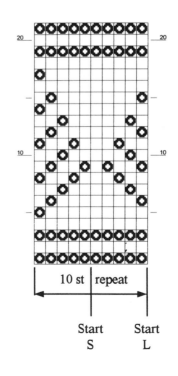

CHART D: YOKE

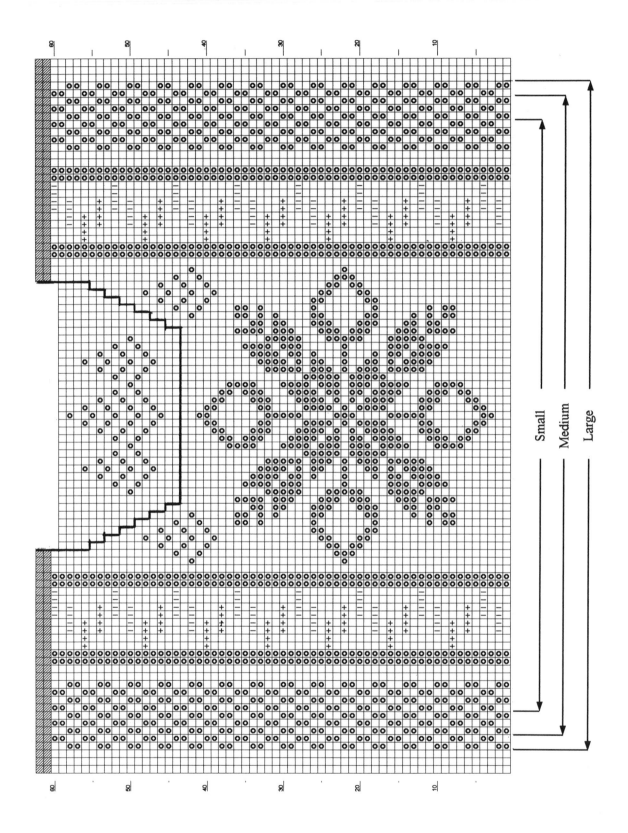

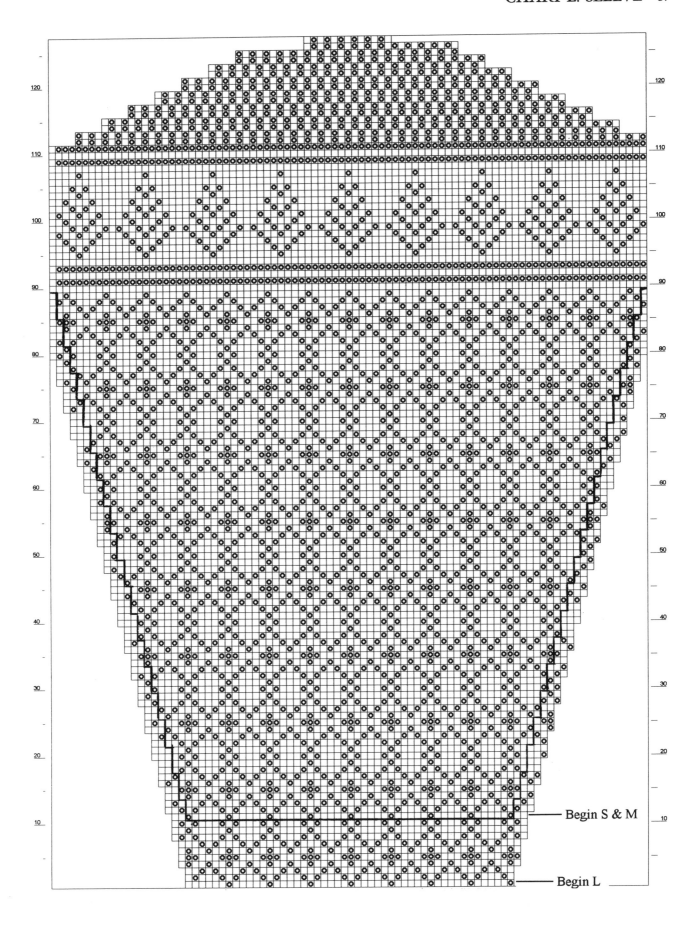

Begin S & M

Begin L

RHAPSODY IN BLUE

This Fair Isle sweater is worked entirely in the round, with steeks for the armholes, front neck, and back neck. All directions for steeking are included in these instructions. For a general explanation of steeking, see the "Tips and Techniques" chapter. (Pictured on page 23.)

YARN: Harrisville Shetland Style (50 gm/1.75 oz skeins)

COLOR	SMALL	LARGE
MC. Oatmeal	8	9
A. Navy	4	5
B. Cobalt	2	3
C. Azure	2	3
D. Wedgewood	2	3
E. Mulberry Tweed	1	1

NEEDLES: Circular #1 and #3 (24-inch), circular #2 and #3 (16-inch), double-pointed #2 and #3.

GAUGE: 27 sts and 31 rows = 4 inches (worked over pattern on #3 needle).

FINISHED CHEST SIZES. Small: 41.5 inches; Large: 50 inches.

(For information on converting measurements and needle sizes to metric equivalents, see page 33.)

PATTERN. Stockinette Stitch: Knit every round.

BODY: With #1 circular needle and COLOR A, cast on 280–336 sts. Join and place a marker. All rnds begin and end at this marker. Work the following 4 rnds 7–8 times.

Rnds 1 and 2: Purl.
Rnds 3 and 4: Knit.

Change to #3 needle and begin CHART A, working the 28-st repeat indicated for your size 10–12 times around the body of the sweater. Work the 40 rnds of the chart 3–4 times. (120–160 rnds total.)

On the last rnd of the last chart repeat, work 140–168 sts, place a marker, work to end of rnd. This divides your work into front and back.

DIVIDE FOR ARMHOLES AND BEGIN STEEKS:
On this rnd you will be casting on your steek stitches. These 10 extra stitches form a bridge where the armhole openings will be, and allow work to continue in the round. Later on, these steek stitches will be cut up the middle to form the armhole opening, trimmed, and hemmed down. The sleeve stitches will be picked up around this opening.

Following rnd 1 of CHART A and beginning at marker *work to 6 sts before next marker, place the next 13 sts on a pin, place a marker, cast on 10 steek sts, alternating colors, place a marker,* repeat between *s. You will now be working on 127–155 sts each for the front and back.

Continue working the steek stitches in alternating colors on subsequent rnds, reversing the order on each rnd. Ends do not need to be worked in anymore, since the steek will be cut and the ends trimmed away. All rnds begin and end at st #5 of the steek, and this is where all new colors will be joined in.

Work rnds 2–40 of CHART B, then repeat rnds 1–7 again. *Remember:* Begin at line indicated for your size, work to end of the repeat for your size, then work the entire 28-st repeat. Front and back are worked the same.

SHAPE NECK: Following rnd 1 of CHART C, work 44–58 sts, put middle 39 sts on a holder for front neck, place a marker, cast on 10 sts for front neck steek, alternating colors, place a marker, work remaining 44–58 sts of front. Work the 127–155 sts of back. This front neck steek is worked exactly the same as the armhole steeks.

Continue working the armhole steeks and the front neck steek. The back is worked straight until shortly before the end. You will begin shaping the back neck while you are still shaping the front neck.

Front Neck: Decrease 1 st each side of neck every rnd 5 times. Decreases are worked as follows: Work to 2 sts before front neck steek, K2 together, work the 10 steek sts, SSK, work remaining sts.

Work 1 rnd. Beginning on the next rnd, decrease 1 st at each side of neck every 3rd rnd 6 times. Work 2 rnds. *At the same time,* begin back neck shaping where indicated on the chart.

Rnd 26: On last round of front, cast off 5 steek sts of armhole at beginning of rnd, work sts of front, casting off 10 front neck steek sts, work to armhole steek, cast off 10 armhole steek sts, work sts of back, cast off remaining 5 steek sts of armhole. Place 33–47 sts on holders for shoulders.

Back Neck. *Note: Back is worked 1 more row than front.* On the rnd 19 of Chart C, work 40–54 sts of back, place middle 47 sts on a holder for back neck, place a marker, cast on 10 steek sts alternating colors, place a marker, work remaining 40–54 sts of back. This back steek is worked the same as armhole and front neck steeks. Work 1 rnd, then decrease 1 st each side of neck every rnd 7 times. Decreases are worked same as front neck steek.

Rnd 27: On last rnd of back, attach yarn to right armhole. Work to 2 sts before steek, K2 together, cast off 9 steek sts, K2 together, bind off last steek st over this K2 together stitch, work remaining sts. Place 33–47 sts on holders for shoulders.

CUTTING THE STEEKS: Using the zigzag stitch on a sewing machine, or backstitching by hand, sew through all cast-on and cast-off edges of all steeks. Using a sharp pair of scissors, cut up the middle of the steeks between sts 5 and 6. Trim away ends left from changing colors.

While most directions for steeking call for trimming them down to a 2-st width, I prefer the security of keeping them at 5 sts. Turn back the 5 steek sts, hemming them down by hand using an overcast stitch. Be careful that your stitching does not show through on the right side. When you have finished, work back over the stitches in the opposite direction, forming Xs.

Steam gently.

JOIN SHOULDERS: Use the knitted seam method.

NECK. Note: When picking up sts around openings that have been steeked, use the st directly adjacent to the last steek st. Insert the needle through both loops of the st, draw yarn through, and knit.

With right side facing and starting at left shoulder seam, using #2 (16-inch) circular needle and COLOR A, pick up and knit 28 sts down left front, knit 39 sts from front neck holder, pick up and knit 28 sts. up right front neck to shoulder seam, pick up and knit 10 sts down right back, knit the 47 sts from back neck holder, pick up and knit 10 sts up left back. (162 sts.)

Rnds. 1 and 2: Purl
Rnds. 3 and 4: Knit
Work these 4 rnds 3 times (12 rnds total), de-

creasing 22 sts on the last rnd. Decrease rnd is worked as follows: K7, K2 together, *K5, K2 together*, repeat between *s 21 times, end K6. (140 sts.) Work in K1, P1 ribbing for 1.5 inches. Bind off in rib.

SLEEVES: Work begins on rnd 32 on fourth st from right side of CHART D. Begin at vertical lines, work to end of stitch repeat, then work full 28-st repeat. Work the vertical lines in numerical order. *Note: Decreases are shown only for beginning of rnd. Do not forget to do them at end of rnd also.*

With 16-inch #3 needle and MC, knit last 6 sts from underarm pin, pick up and knit 75 sts to shoulder seam, pick up and knit another 75 sts to underarm pin, knit 6 sts from pin, place a marker, knit last st, place a marker. (163 sts.) The st between the markers is the underarm st, and is always knit in MC. All decreasing is done on either side of this st as follows: K2 together at beginning of rnd, work to 2 sts before marker, SSK, K underarm st.

Following Chart D, decrease 1 st at beginning and end every third rnd 37–41 times. (89–81 sts.) Change to double-pointed needles when necessary. Work even through rnd 27–7.

Change to #2 double-pointed needles and work 1 rnd in COLOR A, decreasing 41–27 sts evenly spaced. (48–54 sts.) Continue in COLOR A, working K1, P1 ribbing for 3 inches. Bind off in rib.

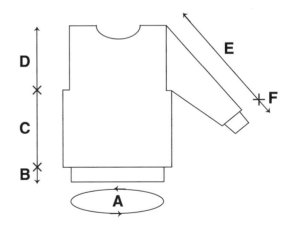

MEASUREMENTS (in inches)
    A. 41.5–50
    B. 2.25–2.5
    C. 15.5–20.5
    D. 9.5
    E. 15–17.5
    F. 3

CHART A: BODY
(Pattern Repeats)

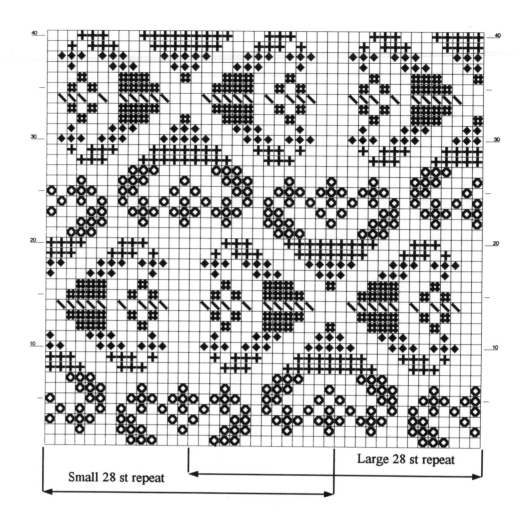

CHART C: NECK SHAPING
(Left Side)

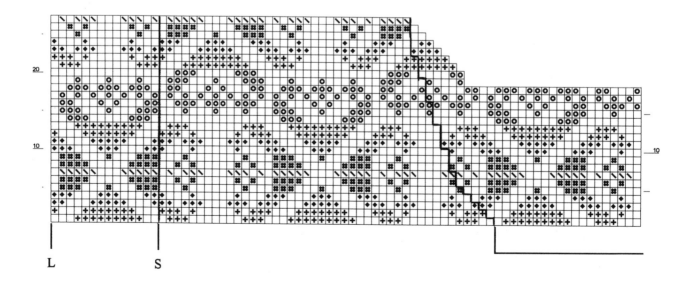

CHART B:
ARMHOLES

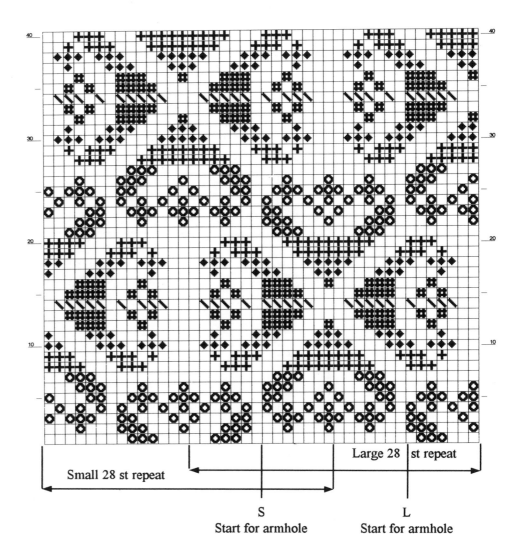

Small 28 st repeat

Large 28 st repeat

S
Start for armhole

L
Start for armhole

KEY FOR CHARTS

- A. Navy
- B. Cobalt
- C. Azure
- D. Wedgwood
- E. Mulberry Tweed
- MC. Oatmeal

CHART C: NECK SHAPING
(Right Side)

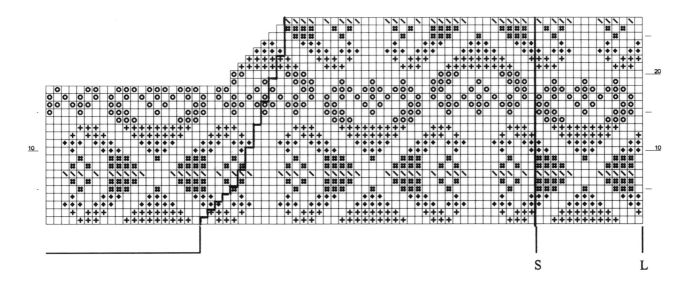

S   L

CHART D: SLEEVE

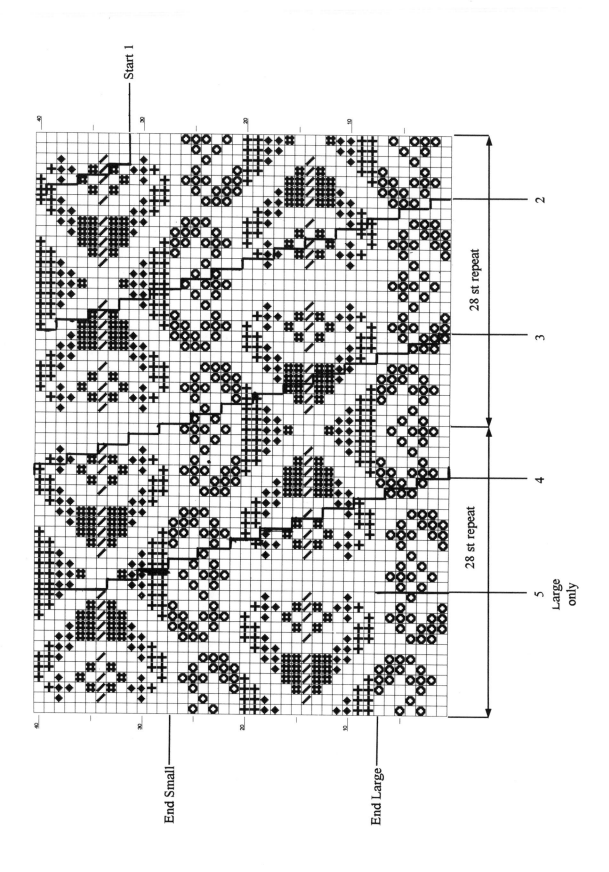

⊞ NORWEGIAN PULLOVER

This pullover is worked entirely in the round, with steeks for the armholes, front neck, and back neck. The two-color braid around the bottom, neck, and sleeves is a technique that is often used on Latvian mittens. All directions for steeking are included in these instructions. For a general explanation of steeking, see the "Tips and Techniques" chapter. (Pictured on page 20.)

YARN: Harrisville Shetland style (50 gm/1.75 oz skeins)

COLOR	SMALL	MED.	LARGE
A. Midnight Blue	8	8	9
B. White	4	4	5
C. Chianti	1	1	1

NEEDLES: #1, #2, #3 circular (24-inch), #2 and #3 double-pointed, #2 circular (16-inch)

GAUGE: 27 sts and 31 rows = 4 inches (worked over pattern on #3 needles).

FINISHED CHEST SIZES (in inches)

Small	42.5
Medium	45
Large	47.5

(For information on converting measurements and needle sizes to metric equivalents, see page 33.)

PATTERNS

Stockinette Stitch: Knit every round.

Two-Color Braid: See instructions for rounds 1 through 3 of body.

BODY: With #1 circular needle and COLOR A, cast on 288–304–320 sts. Place a marker and join. All rnds begin and end at this marker. Knit 3 rnds, then work one rnd of *K2 together, YO*, repeat between *s. Change to #2 needle and knit 2 rnds, then work the 3 rnds of two-color braid as follows:

Rnd. 1: *K1 COLOR A, K1 COLOR B*, repeat between *s.

Rnd. 2: Bring both colors forward. *P1 Color A, P1 Color B*, repeat between *s. Always bring the next color to purl over the yarn from the previous stitch. The two colors of yarn will twist around each other. The next round will untwist them, but on the longer rnds (as on the body) you may want to hang your work and spin it to untwist the yarn.

Rnd. 3: *P 1 Color A, P 1 Color B*, repeat between *s, but bring the next color *under* the yarn from the previous stitch.

Knit two rnds in COLOR A.

Change to #3 circular needle, and, following CHART A, work the 8-st repeat for your size 36–38–40 times around the body of the sweater. Work rnds 1 through 28, then repeat rnds 29 through 36 another 8–9–11 times.

Note: The rnd numbers used from here on are *chart numbers*, not actual number of rnds completed.

Work rnds 37–44 of Chart A.

On rnd 45, work 144–152–160 sts, place a marker, work to end of rnd. This divides your work into front and back.

DIVIDE FOR ARMHOLES AND BEGIN STEEKS: On rnd 46 of Chart A, you will be casting on your steek stitches. These 10 extra stitches form a bridge where the armhole openings will be, and allow work to continue in the round. Later on, these steek stitches will be cut up the middle to form the armhole opening, trimmed, and hemmed down. The sleeve stitches will be picked up around this opening.

Beginning at marker, *work to 9 sts before next marker, place the next 17 sts on a pin*, place a marker, cast on 10 steek sts in alternating colors, place a marker, repeat between *s, place a marker, cast on 5 sts in alternating colors, change to colors used in rnd 1 of CHART B, cast on 5 sts in alternating colors, place a marker.

You will now be working on 127–135–143 sts each for the front and back. Ends do not need to be worked in anymore, since the steek will be cut and the ends trimmed away. All rnds begin and end at st #5 of the steek, and this is where all new colors will be joined in. Work all steeks in alternating colors, reversing the order on each rnd.

Work rnds 1–45 of Chart B.

SHAPE NECK: Following rnd 46 of Chart B, work 52–56–60 sts, place middle 23 sts onto a holder for front neck, place a marker, cast on 10 steek sts for front neck in alternating colors, place a marker, work to end of rnd. This front neck steek is worked exactly the same as the armhole steeks.

Continue working the armhole steeks and the front neck steek. The back is worked straight until shortly before the end. *You will begin shaping the back neck while you are still shaping the front neck.*

FRONT NECK: Decrease 1 st each side of front neck every rnd 7 times, every other rnd 3 times, then every 3rd. rnd 2 times. *Note:* Even though the chart shows pattern symbols on the stitches directly adjacent to neck, always work these sts in Color A. Decreases are worked on either side of the neck steek as follows: K2 together, work 10 steek sts, SSK.

Work 2-2-9 rnds even.

BACK NECK: Begin back neck shaping on rnd 61–61–68. Work 46–50–54 sts of back, place middle 35 sts on holder for back neck, place a marker, cast on 10 steek sts in alternating colors, place a marker, work to end of rnd. This back steek is worked the same as armhole and front neck steek. Beginning on next rnd, decrease 1 st each side of back neck steek every rnd 5 times (decreases are worked same as for front neck steek.).

The sixth, and last, back neck decrease rnd is worked on rnd 67–67–74. Work first 5 steek sts at beginning of rnd, work all sts of front to 2nd armhole steek stitches, cast off these 10 steek sts, work to 2 sts before back neck steek, K2 together, cast off 9 back neck steek sts, K2 together, cast off last steek st over this K2 together. Work remaining sts of back, cast off 10 armhole steek sts.

LAST ROW OF FRONT: Work rnd 68–68–75, casting off front neck steek sts. *Note:* Front is worked one more rnd than back.

Put 40–44–48 sts on #3 double-pointed needles for front and back shoulders.

CUTTING THE STEEKS: Using the zigzag stitch on a sewing machine, or backstitching by hand, sew through all cast-on and cast-off edges of all steeks. Using a sharp pair of scissors, cut up the middle of the steeks between sts 5 and 6. Trim away ends left from changing colors.

While most directions for steeking call for trimming them down to a 2-stitch width, I prefer the security of keeping them at 5 stitches. Turn back the 5 steek sts, hemming them down by hand using an overcast stitch. Be careful that your stitching does not show through on the right side. When you have finished, work back over the stitches in the opposite direction, forming Xs.

Steam gently.

JOIN SHOULDER: Use the knitted seam method.

COLLAR. *Note:* When picking up stitches around openings that have been steeked, use the stitch directly adjacent to the last steek stitch. Insert the needle through both loops of the stitch, draw yarn through, and knit.

With right side facing and starting at right shoulder seam, using COLOR A and #3 double-pointed needles, pick up and knit 8 sts along back right neck, knit 35 sts from back neck holder, pick up and knit 8 sts along left back neck to shoulder, pick up and knit 23–23–31 sts along left front, knit 23 sts from front neck holder, pick up and knit 23–23–31 sts along right front to shoulder seam. (120–120–136 sts.)

Work 1 rnd in Color A.

Work the 7 rnds of CHART C, working the 8-st repeat 15–15–17 times around neck.

Change to #2 needles and work 2 rnds in COLOR A.

Work the 3 rnds of two-color braid as for body.

Work 2 rnds in Color A, then one rnd of *K2 together, YO*, repeat between *s.

Work 13 rnds, decreasing 3 sts evenly spaced on the fifth rnd.

Bind off. Fold at the K2 tog, YO rnd and turn under. Slip stitch in place.

Turn under hem for body in the same way.

SLEEVES: With #3 double-pointed needles and COLOR A, knit the last 8 sts from underarm pin, pick up and knit 68–68–76 sts to shoulder, pick up and knit another 68–68–76 sts to pin. Knit 8 sts from pin, place a marker, knit last st, place a marker. (153–153–169 sts.)

The stitch between the markers is the underarm st, and is always knit in Color A. All decreasing is done on either side of this st as follows: K2 tog at beginning of rnd, work to 2 sts before marker, SSK, knit underarm st.

To Read Sleeve Chart: CHART D is divided into two portions. Since the sleeve will be knit from the shoulder down to the wrist, begin with the "Upper Sleeve" portion of the chart. Work begins on first stitch at right side of the chart. Begin at vertical line labeled "Start," work to end of stitch repeat, then work full 8-st repeats across the rnd. As you progress up the chart, work the vertical (decrease) lines in numerical order. *Remember: Decrease lines on sleeve chart are shown only for the beginning of the rnd. Do not forget to work decreases at the end of the rnd also!*

Following Chart D (Upper Sleeve), work rnds 1 and 2, then repeat rnds 3 through 10 another 12–12–14 times.

Then, following Lower Sleeve portion of Chart D, work rnds 11 through 46. Decrease 1 st at beginning and 1 st at end of every second rnd 13 times, every third rnd 2 times, every fourth rnd 4 times, then every fifth rnd 17 times. Work 1–1–17 rnds even, ending with a completed rnd 46. (81–81–97 sts.)

Change to #2 needles. Work 2 rnds in Color A. Work the 3 rnds of two-color braid as for body.

Work 2 rnds of Color A, decreasing 1 st on the last rnd. (80–80–96 sts.)

Work 1 rnd of *K2 together, YO*, repeat between * to end of round. Knit 10 rnds for hem, decreasing 2 sts at underarm st (as for sleeve) on rnd 7. (78–78–94 sts.) Bind off loosely.

Turn under hem as for neck and body.

FINISHING: Weave in any loose ends. Steam lightly.

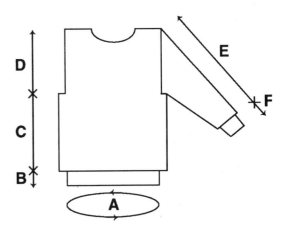

MEASUREMENTS (in inches)

A. 42.5–45–47.5	D. 9–9–10
B. no ribbing	E. 17–17–19
C. 14.5–15.5–16.5	

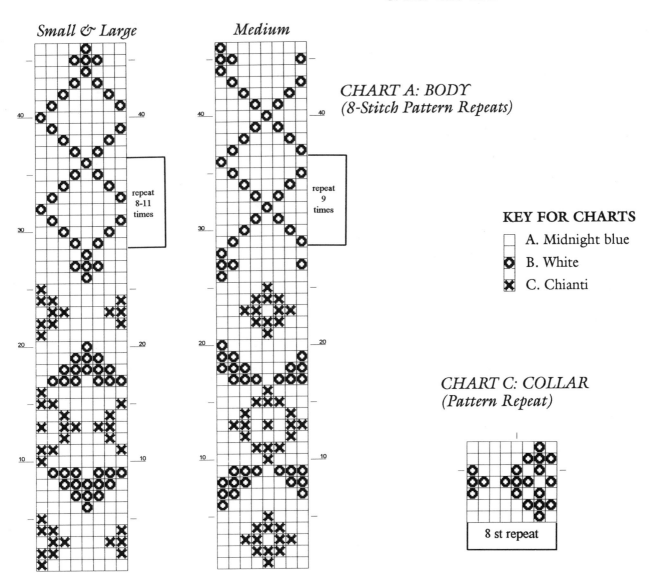

Small & Large

Medium

repeat 8-11 times

repeat 9 times

CHART A: BODY
(8-Stitch Pattern Repeats)

KEY FOR CHARTS

☐ A. Midnight blue
◉ B. White
✖ C. Chianti

CHART C: COLLAR
(Pattern Repeat)

8 st repeat

CHART B: YOKE MOTIF & NECK SHAPING

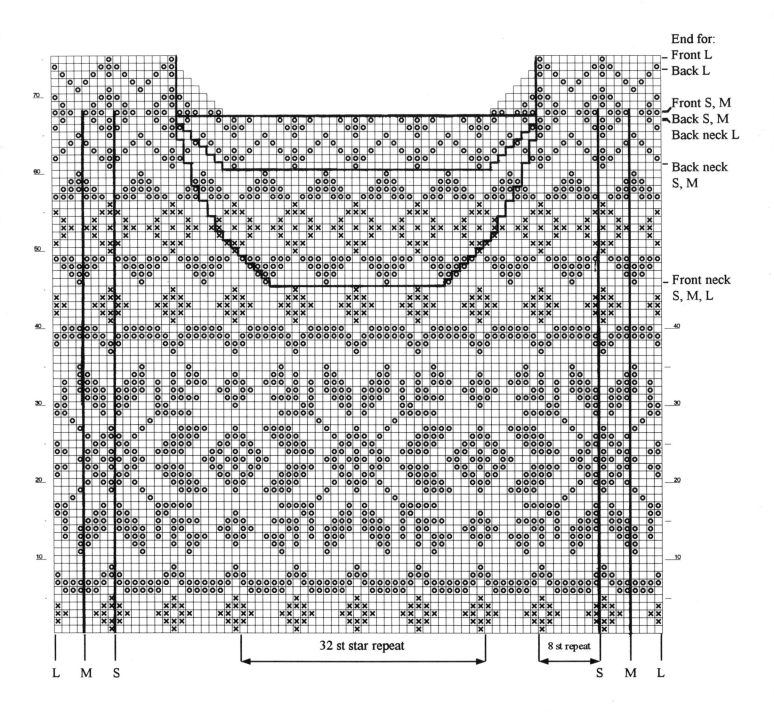

End for:
– Front L
– Back L

Front S, M
Back S, M
Back neck L

– Back neck S, M

– Front neck S, M, L

32 st star repeat

8 st repeat

L M S   S M L

CHART D: LOWER SLEEVE

8 st repeats

L   S&M

CHART D: UPPER SLEEVE

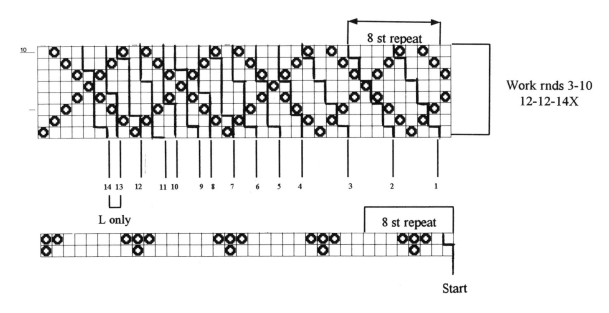

8 st repeat

Work rnds 3-10
12-12-14X

14 13 12 11 10 9 8 7 6 5 4   3   2   1

L only

8 st repeat

Start

❖ OWL EYES FAIR ISLE

The light stripe through the pattern of this sweater reminded my children of owls' eyes. The entire sweater is knit in the round, with steeks for the armholes, front neck, and back neck. All directions for steeking are included in these instructions. For a general explanation of steeking, see the "Tips and Techniques" chapter. (Pictured on page 14.)

YARN: Harrisville Shetland Style (50 gm/1.75 oz skeins)

COLOR	SMALL	MED.	LARGE
A. Ebony Tweed	2	2	3
B. Dawn Mist	2	2	3
C. Burgundy Tweed	1	1	1
D. Silver Mauve	1	1	1
E. Loden Blue	4	4	4
F. Turquoise Tweed	2	2	2
G. Aqua Blue	2	2	2
H. Seam Mist	1	1	1

NEEDLES: Circular #2 and #3 (24-inch), double-pointed #2 and #3

GAUGE: 29 sts and 28 rows = 4 inches (worked over pattern on #3 needle).

FINISHED SIZES (in inches)

Small	36.5
Medium	42.5
Large	48.5

(For information on converting measurements and needle sizes to metric equivalents, see page 33.)

PATTERNS
Corrugated Rib: K2 in one color; P2 in other color
Stockinette Stitch: Knit every round.

BODY: With #2 circular needle and COLOR A, cast on 220–264–308 sts. Join and place a marker. All rnds begin and end at this marker. Work in corrugated rib in the following color/rnd sequences for 28–28–33 rnds.

	COLORS		# OF RNDS.	
	K2	P2	SM. & MED.	LGE.
Sequence I	A	B	3	3
	C	D	2	2
	A	B	3	3
	E	F	3	4
	E	G	2	3
Sequence II	E	H	2	

Now repeat Sequence I (first 5 lines of table) in reverse order.

Next rnd: Change to #3 circular needle and knit one rnd with COLOR A, increasing 44 sts evenly spaced. *For size Small,* *K5, inc 1*. *For Medium,* *K6, inc. 1*. *For Large,* *K7, inc.1*. Repeat between *s across rnd. (264–308–352 sts.)

Following CHART A, work the 22-st repeat indicated for your size 12–14–16 times around the body of the sweater, beginning on rnd 1–12–1. *Size Small:* Repeat the 24 rnds of the chart 3 times. *Size Medium:* Work rnds 12–24, then repeat the 24 rnds of the chart 3 times. *Size Large:* Repeat the 24 rnds of the chart 4 times. (72–84–96 rnds.)

On the last rnd of the last chart repeat, work 132–154–176 sts, place a marker, work to end of rnd. This divides your work into front and back.

DIVIDE FOR ARMHOLES AND BEGIN STEEKS: On the next rnd (rnd 1 of Chart B) you will be casting on your steek stitches. These 10 extra stitches form a bridge where the armhole openings will be, and allow work to continue in the round. Later on, these steek stitches will be cut up the middle to form the armhole opening, trimmed, and hemmed down. The sleeve stitches will be picked up around this opening.

Beginning at first stitch of repeat for your size on rnd 1 of CHART B, and beginning at marker, *work to 3 sts before next marker, place the next 7 sts on a pin*, place a marker, cast on 10 steek sts in alternating colors, place a marker, repeat between *s, place a marker, cast on 5 steek sts in alternating colors, change to colors used on rnd 2 of Chart B, cast on 5 stitches in alternating colors, place a marker. You will now be working on 125–147–169 sts each for the front and back.

Continue working the steek stitches in alternating colors on subsequent rnds, reversing the order on each rnd. Ends do not need to be worked in anymore, since the steek will be cut and the ends trimmed away. All rnds begin and end at st #5 of the steek, and this is where all new colors will be joined in.

Armhole Shaping: Beginning on rnd 2 of Chart B, decrease one stitch each side of each armhole steek on the next 5 rnds (115–137–159 sts each for front and back.)

Decreases are worked as follows: Work 5 steek sts, K2 together, work to within 2 sts of next steek, SSK, work 10 steek sts, K2 together, work to within 2 sts of next steek, SSK, work last 5 steek sts. Remember to begin the rnd at the decrease line, working to the end of the 22 st repeat for your size, then working all subsequent repeats the full 22 sts of the repeat for your size. *Decreases on chart are shown only at beginning of armholes; do not forget to do them on the other armhole side of front and back.* Decreasing is done 4 times in each round.

Work even for the remaining 18 rnds of Chart B. Work the 24 rnds of CHART C.

SHAPE NECK: Working from CHART D, work 0–0–8 rnds. On rnd 1–1–9, work 44–55–62 sts, place middle 27–27–35 sts on a holder for front neck, place a marker, cast on 10 sts in alternating colors for front neck steek, place a marker, work remaining 44–55–62 sts of front. Work the 115–137–159 sts of back. This front neck steek is worked exactly the same as the armhole steeks. Continue working the armhole steeks and the front neck steek. The back is worked straight until shortly before the end. You will begin shaping the back neck while still working the front neck and armhole steeks.

Front Neck: Decrease 1 st each side of neck every other rnd 7–7–9 times. Decreases are worked as follows: Work to within 2 sts of neck steek, K2 together, knit the 10 steek sts, SSK, work remaining sts of front. Work 4 rnds even, then begin back neck shaping while still working on 37–48–53 sts for each front shoulder.

Back Neck: On rnd 20–20–32, work 40–51–56 sts, place the middle 35–35–47 sts on a holder for back neck, place a marker, cast on 10 steek sts in alternating colors, place a marker, work remaining 40–51–56 sts. This back steek is worked the same as armhole and front neck steeks. Decrease 1 st at each side of back neck edge every rnd 3 times. (37–48–53 sts for each shoulder) Decreases are worked the same as front neck.

Rnd 24–24–36: Work first 5 steek sts at beginning of round, work all stitches of front and the second armhole steek sts, work 37–48–53 sts of back, cast off the ten steek sts of back neck, work remaining 37–48–53 sts of back, cast off the last 5 steek sts of rnd.

Rnd 25–25–37: *Front only* (front is worked one more rnd than back). Cast off first 5 steek sts, work 37–48–53 sts of front, cast off the ten steek sts of front neck, work remaining 37–48–53 sts, cast off the 10 steek sts of second armhole. Place each set of shoulder sts on a #5 double-pointed needle.

CUTTING THE STEEKS: Using the zigzag stitch on a sewing machine, or backstitching by hand, sew through the cast-on and cast-off edges of all steeks. Using a sharp pair of scissors, cut up the middle of the steeks between sts #5 and #6. Trim away ends left from changing colors.

While most directions for steeking call for trimming them down to a 2-stitch width, I prefer the security of keeping them at 5 stitches. Turn back the 5 steek sts, hemming them down by hand using an overcast stitch. Be careful that your stitching does not show through on the right side. When you have finished, work back over the stitches in the opposite direction, forming Xs.

Steam gently.

JOIN SHOULDERS: Use the knitted seam method.

NECK. *Note:* When picking up stitches around openings that have been steeked, use the stitch directly adjacent to the last steek stitch. Insert the needle through both loops of the stitch, draw yarn through, and knit.

With #2 double-pointed needles and COLOR E, and with right side facing, starting at right shoulder, pick up and knit 6 sts down right back, knit 35–35–47 sts from back neck holder, pick up and knit 6–6–6 up left back to shoulder seam, pick up and knit 25–25–29 sts down left front, knit 27–27–35 sts from front neck holder, pick up and knit 25–25–29 sts up right front. Place a marker. (124–124–152 sts.) Work in corrugated rib in the following color/rnd sequence. (10–10–10 rnds.)

COLOR		
K2	P2	# OF RNDS
E	H	2
E	G	2
E	F	2
A	B	2
C	D	1
A	B	1

Bind off loosely in knit using COLOR A.

SLEEVES: With #3 double-pointed needles and COLOR D–D–F and starting at underarm pin, knit last 3 sts from pin. Pick up and knit 73–73–85 sts to shoulder seam, pick up and knit another 73–73–85 sts to underarm pin, knit 3 sts from pin, place a marker, knit last st from pin, place a marker. (153–153–177 sts.) This last st between markers is the underarm st and is always worked in the background color. All decreases are made in either side of this stitch as follows: K2 together at beginning of rnd, work to within 2 sts of marker, SSK, knit underarm stitch in background color.

To read the sleeve chart: Work begins on the first st at the right side of the chart. Vertical lines indicate decreases. Begin at vertical line #1, work to end of stitch repeat, then work the full 22-st repeat. Work the vertical lines in numerical order. *Remember: Decrease lines on sleeve chart are shown only at the beginning of the rnd; do not forget to work decreases at the end of the rnd also.*

Following CHART E or F for your size, work 1 round, then decrease 1 st at beginning of round and 1 st at end of rnd every other rnd 10 times, then every third rnd 25–27–30 times. Work 2–8–6 rnds even, ending on rnd 1–12–20. (97–109–116 rnds; 83–79–97 sts.)

Next rnd: Using COLOR A, knit, decreasing 19–11–21 sts evenly spaced. (64–68–76 sts.) Change to #2 double-pointed needles and work corrugated ribbing in same rnd/color sequence as for body. Bind off loosely in knit using Color A.

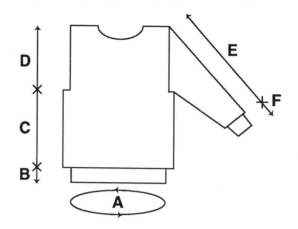

MEASUREMENTS (in inches)
A. 36.5–42.5–48.5
B. 3.25–3.25–3.75
C. 10.25–12–13.75
D. 10.5–10.5–12
E. 14–15.5–16.5
F. 3.25–3.25–3.75

CHART A: LOWER BODY
(Pattern Repeats)

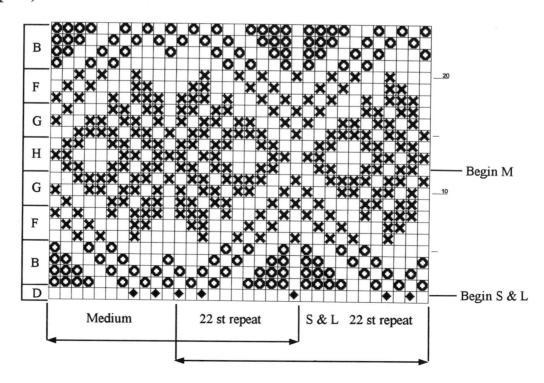

CHART B: ARMHOLES

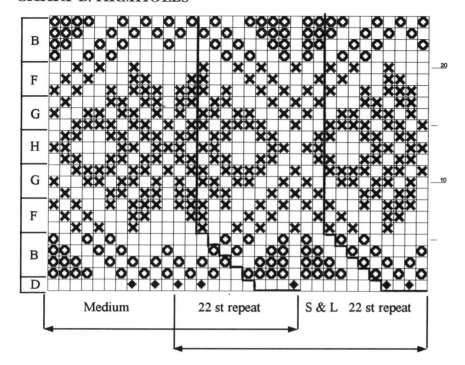

Medium   22 st repeat   S & L   22 st repeat

KEY FOR CHARTS

◉	A. Ebony Tweed
◆	C. Burgundy Tweed
✕	E. Loden Blue
☐	background color

CHART C: UPPER BODY

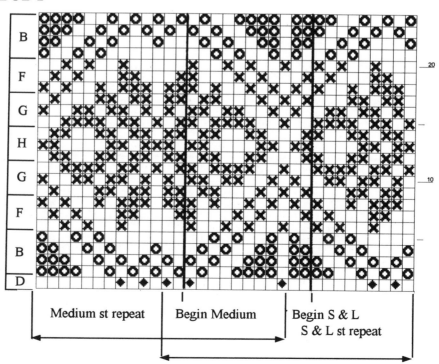

Medium st repeat   Begin Medium   Begin S & L
S & L st repeat

CHART D: NECK SHAPING
(Left Side)

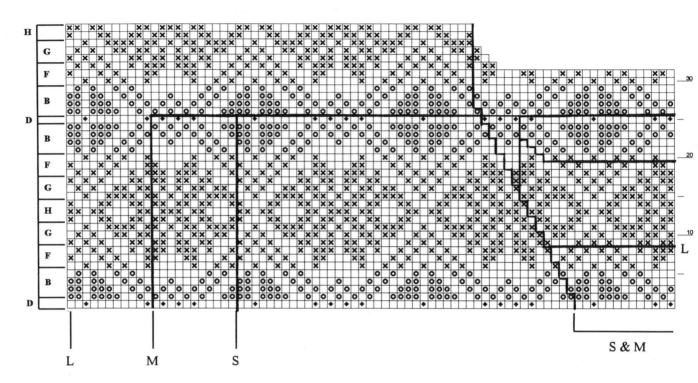

CHART E: SLEEVE (Large)

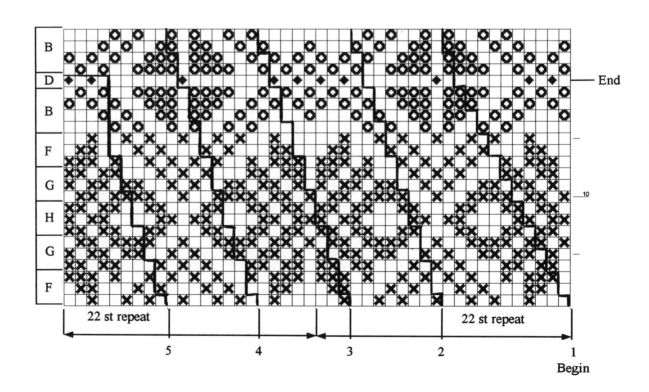

CHART D: NECK SHAPING
(Right Side)

End for:
Front L
Back L

Front S, M
Back S, M

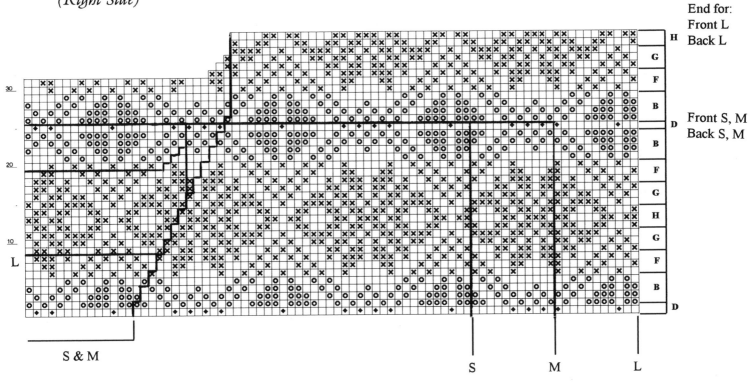

S & M

S M L

CHART F: SLEEVE *(Medium & Small)*

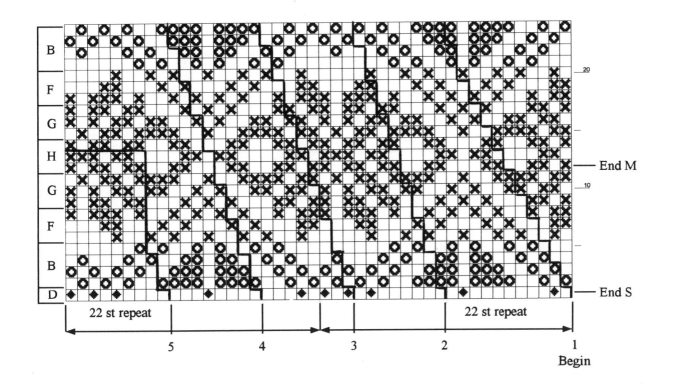

End M

End S

22 st repeat   22 st repeat

5   4   3   2   1

Begin

BLACKBERRY & LICHEN

A chevron design worked as a border on the body, sleeves, and around the neck provides a point of contrasting interest in this tunic-style sweater. Using only two colors, the work progresses quickly and easily. This sweater is worked entirely in the round, with steeks for the armholes, front neck, and back neck. All directions for steeking are included in these instructions. For a general explanation of steeking, see the "Tips and Techniques" chapter. (Pictured on page 17.)

YARN: Harrisville Shetland Style (50 gm/1.75 oz skeins)

COLOR	SMALL	MED.	LARGE
A. Blackberry	5	6	8
B. Lichen	5	6	8

NEEDLES: Circular #1 and #3 (24-inch), circular #3 (16-inch), double-pointed #1 and #3

GAUGE: 27 sts and 31 rnds = 4 inches (worked over pattern on #3 needle).

FINISHED CHEST SIZES

Small	39 inches
Medium	45.5 inches
Large	52.25 inches

(For information on converting measurements and needle sizes to metric equivalents, see page 33.)

PATTERN. Stockinette Stitch: Knit every round.

BODY: With 24-inch #1 circular needle and COLOR A, cast on 264–308–352 sts. Place a marker and join. All rnds begin and end at this marker. Work the following 6 rnds.

Rnds 1 and 2: Purl.
Rnds 3 and 4: Knit.
Rnds 5 and 6: Purl.

Next rnd: Still using Color A, knit 132–154–176 sts, place a marker, knit remaining 132–154–176 sts. This divides your work into front and back. Keep these markers on your needle until you reach armhole divide.

Change to #3 needle. Work the 11 rnds of CHART A as follows for border: *Work the 4-st repeat for your size 14–17–20 times, work the middle 21–19–17 sts for your size, work the next 4-st repeat for your size 13–16–19 times, then the first 3 sts of that repeat*. Slip marker. Repeat between *s for back.

Change to #1 needle and work the following 8 rnds in COLOR A.

Rnd 1: Knit.
Rnds 2 and 3: Purl.
Rnds 4 and 5: Knit.
Rnds 6 and 7: Purl.
Rnd 8: Knit.

Change to #3 needle and CHART B. Beginning on rnd 13–1–37, work the 22-st repeat indicated for your size 12–14–16 times around the body. Work through rnd 48, then repeat entire 48 rnds of chart 1–1–2 time(s). (84–96–108 rnds.)

Change to CHART C, working first 1–1–7 rnd(s).

DIVIDE FOR ARMHOLES AND BEGIN THE STEEKS: On rnd 2–2–8 of Chart C, you will be casting on your steek stitches. These 10 extra stitches form a bridge where the armhole openings will be, and allow work to continue in the round. Later on, these steek stitches will be cut up the middle to form the armhole opening, trimmed, and hemmed down. The sleeve stitches will be picked up around this opening.

Beginning at marker, * work to 3 sts before next marker, put next 7 sts on a pin, place a marker, cast on 10 stitches in alternating colors, place a marker*, repeat between *s. You will now be working on 125–147–169 sts each for the front and back. All rnds now begin and end at stitch #5 of this steek. Work all steeks stitches in alternating colors, reversing the order on each rnd.

Work even to end of Chart C.

SHAPE FRONT NECK: Change to CHART D, working through rnd 2–2–7. On rnd 3–3–8, work 51–62–73 sts, place middle 23 sts on a holder for front neck, place a marker, cast on 10 steek stitches in alternating colors, place a marker, work remaining 51–62–73 stitches of front, then work the 125–147–169 sts of back.

This front neck steek is worked exactly the same

as the armhole steeks. Continue working the armhole steeks and the front neck steek.

The back is worked straight until shortly before the end. You will begin shaping the back neck while you are still shaping the front neck.

Decrease 1 st each side of front neck steek every rnd 7 times, then every other rnd 3 times, then every third rnd 2–2–5 times (39–50–58 sts for each shoulder). Decreases are worked on the 2 stitches directly adjacent to neck steek on both sides as follows: K2 together, work 10 steek stitches, SSK.

SHAPE BACK NECK: On rnd 18–18–30, work 45–56–64 sts of back, place middle 35–35–41 sts on holder for back neck, place a marker, cast on 10 steek stitches in alternating colors, place a marker, work remaining 45–56–64 sts of back.

The back steek is worked the same as armhole and front neck steek. Decreasing is worked in the same manner as front neck.

Beginning on next rnd, decrease 1 st each side of back neck steek on next 5 rnds.

LAST RND OF BACK: On rnd 24–24–36, work first 5 steek sts, work all sts of front, doing any decreases indicated, cast off the 10 steek stitches at second armhole, work the stitches of back to 2 stitches before back steek, K2 together, cast off 9 steek sts, K2 together, cast off last steek st, work to first armhole steek, cast off these 10 steek stitches.

LAST RND OF FRONT. *Note:* Front is worked one more rnd than back. On rnd 25–25–37, work stitches of front to steek, cast off 10 steek sts, work remaining sts. Put 39–50–58 sts for shoulders on #3 double-pointed needles.

CUTTING STEEKS: Using the zigzag stitch on a sewing machine, or backstitching by hand, sew through all cast-on and cast-off edges of all steeks. Using a sharp pair of scissors, cut up the middle of the steeks between sts #5 and #6. Trim away any ends.

While most directions for steeking call for trimming them down to a 2-stitch width, I prefer the security of keeping them at 5 stitches. Turn back the 5 steek sts, hemming them down by hand using an overcast stitch. Be careful that your stitching does not show through on the right side. When you have finished, work back over the stitches in the opposite direction, forming Xs.

Steam gently.

JOIN SHOULDERS: Use the knitted seam method.

NECK. *Note:* When picking up stitches around

openings that have been steeked, use the stitch directly adjacent to the last steek stitch. Insert the needle through both loops of the stitch, draw yarn through, and knit.

With #1 double-pointed needles and COLOR A, starting at right shoulder, pick up and knit 9 sts down right back, knit 35–35–41 sts from back neck holder, marking off the middle st between two markers, pick up and knit 9 sts up left back to shoulder seam, place a marker for end of back. Pick up and knit 23–23–30 sts down left front, knit the 23 sts from front neck holder, marking off middle st between 2 markers, pick up and knit 23–23–30 sts up right front, place a marker for end of front. (122–122–142 sts.)

Work the following 3 rnds in Color A.

Rnds 1 and 2: Purl.

Rnd 3: Knit, decreasing 1 st 10 sts before end of back neck, and 1 st 10 sts before end of front neck. (120–120–140 sts.)

Neck Border: Change to #3 needles, working the 13 rnds of CHART E (52–52–58 sts for back; 68–68–82 sts for front). Make sure the marked-off center stitch coincides with the center stitch of the chart. Once you have this established, you can remove the markers for these center sts.

Change back to #1 needles, and using COLOR A, knit 1 rnd, purl 2 rnds, bind off loosely in knit.

SLEEVES: With #3 16-inch circular needle and COLOR B, knit last 3 sts from pin, pick up and knit 71–71–77 sts to shoulder seam, pick up and knit 71–71–77 sts to underarm pin, knit 3 sts from pin, place a marker, knit last st. (149–149–161 sts.)

This last stitch is the underarm stitch, and is always knit in Color B. All decreasing is done on either side of this stitch as follows. Beginning of rnd: K2 together. End of rnd: SSK, knit underarm st.

Following CHART F or G, according to your size, work 3 rnds even, then decrease 1 st at beginning and 1 st at end of rnd every fourth rnd 26–29–32 times, ending on rnd 8–20–32. (97–91–97 sts.) *Note:* You will have to switch to #3 double-pointed needles at some point when there are too few stitches for the 16-inch circular needle.

Sleeve Border: Change to #1 needles and begin CHART H. (*Note:* Work underarm stitch in charted pattern for entire 26 rnds of this chart.) Decrease 1 st at beginning and 1 st at end of rnd every third rnd 8–5–3 times. Work 2–11–17 rnds even to end of chart. (81–81–91 sts.) Bind off in knit.

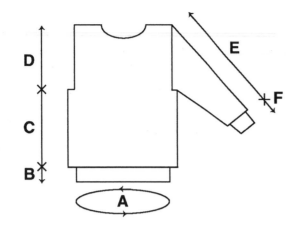

MEASUREMENTS (in inches)
  A. 39–45.5–52.25
  B. 2.5
  C. 11–12.5–14
  D. 9.25–9.25–10
  E. 13.5–15–16.5
  F. 2.5

CHART B: BODY

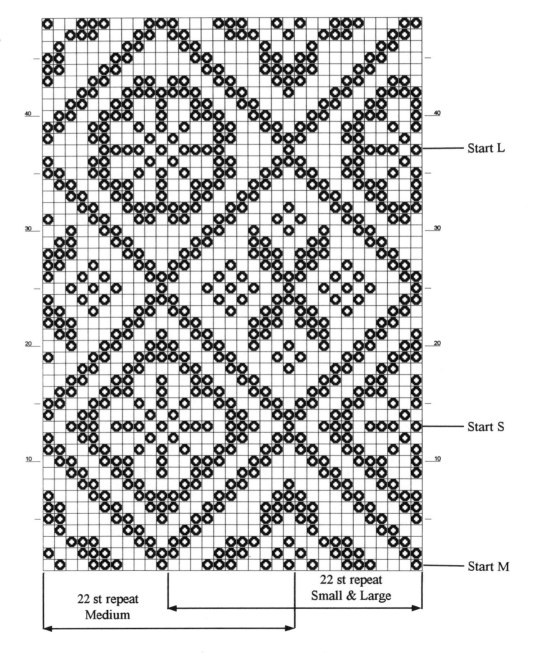

Start L

Start S

Start M

22 st repeat
Small & Large

22 st repeat
Medium

CHART A: BORDER

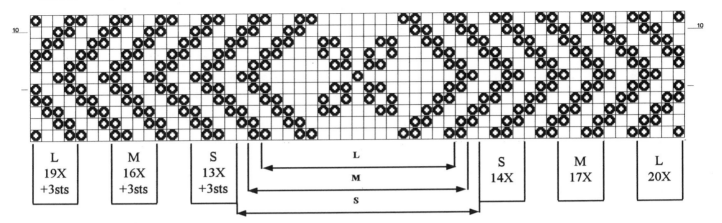

| L 19X +3sts | M 16X +3sts | S 13X +3sts | L / M / S | S 14X | M 17X | L 20X |

CHART C: ARMHOLES

KEY FOR CHARTS
- A. Blackberry
- purl in Blackberry
- B. Lichen

Medium

Small & Large

M

S & L

CHART D: NECK SHAPING (Left Side)

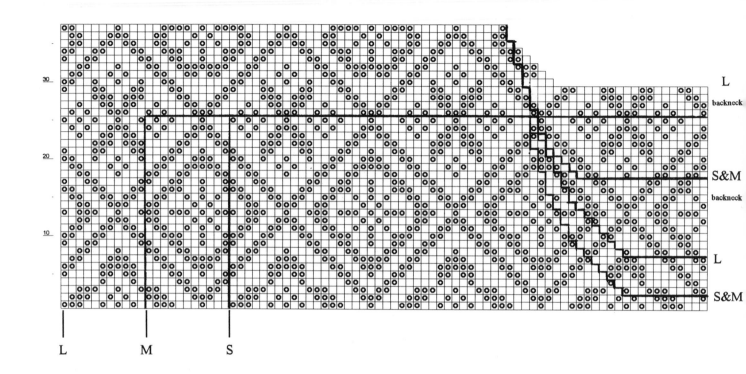

L
backneck

S&M
backneck

L

S&M

L   M   S

CHART F: SLEEVE
(Small & Medium)

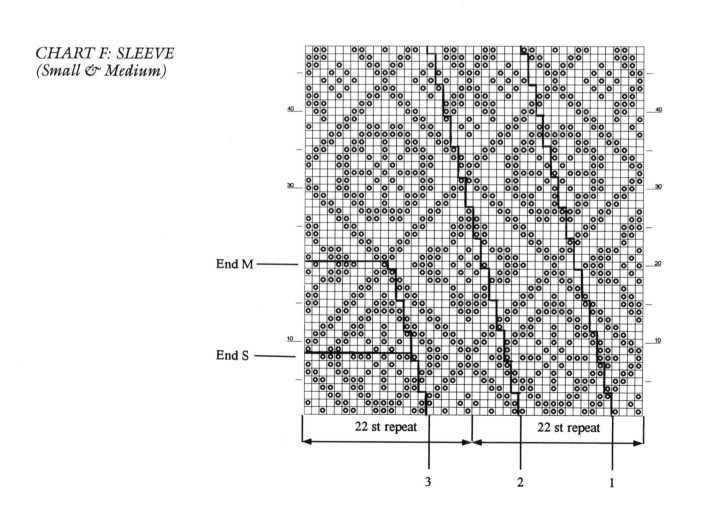

End M ——

End S ——

22 st repeat   22 st repeat

3   2   1

CHART D: NECK SHAPING (Right Side)

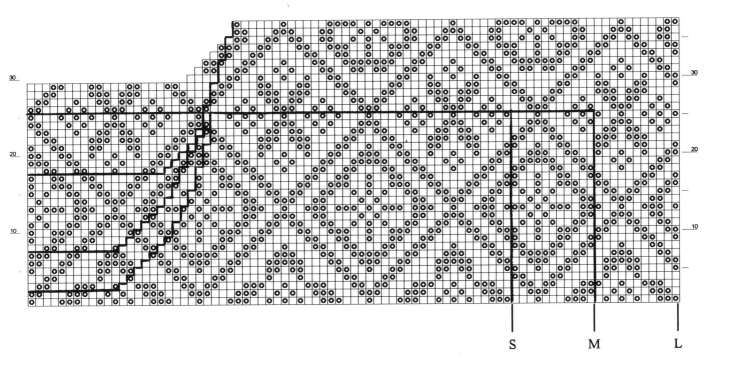

S   M   L

CHART G: SLEEVE
(Large)

End —

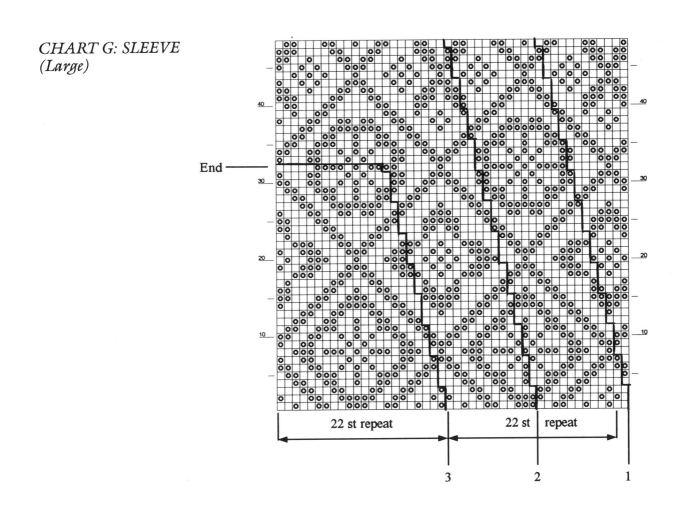

22 st repeat   22 st | repeat

3   2   1

CHART H: SLEEVE BORDER

CHART E: NECK BORDER

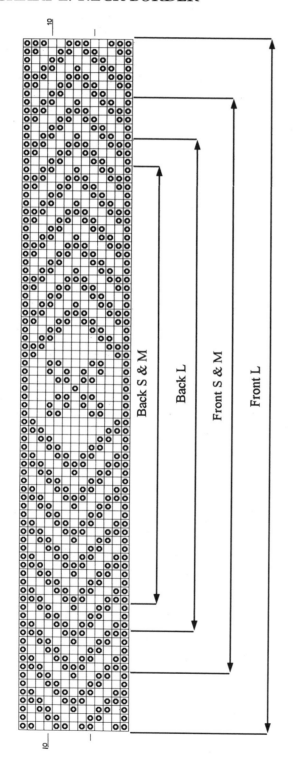

❖ FAIR ISLE BORDER SWEATER

This sweater is a good introduction to Fair Isle technique. The body and sleeves feature a Fair Isle border, and a portion of the border motif is repeated around the neck, but most of the sweater is plain. It is knit in the round up to the armholes. Sleeves are worked in the round, then set into the body. (Pictured on page 25.)

YARN: Harrisville Shetland Style (50gm/1.75 oz skeins)

COLOR	PETITE	SMALL	MED.	LGE.
A. Bottle Green Tw.	6	7	8	9
B. Aubergine	1	1	1	1
C. Periwinkle	1	1	1	1
D. Lavender	1	1	1	1
E. Silver Mauve	1	1	1	1
F. Cornsilk (few yds.)	1	1	1	1

NEEDLES: Circular #2, #3, and #4 (24-inch); circular #2 and #4 (16-inch); #2, #3, and #4 double-pointed; #3 straight .

GAUGE: 23 sts and 32 rows = 4 inches (worked in stockinette stitch on #3 needles).

FINISHED CHEST SIZES (in inches)

Petite	37
Small	42
Medium	47
Large	52

(For information on converting measurements and needle sizes to metric equivalents, see page 33.)

PATTERN: Stockinette Stitch (K one row, P one row, when working back and forth; K every round, when working on circular needle).

BODY: With 24-inch #2 circular needle and COLOR A, cast on 210–240–270–300 sts. Join and place a marker. All rnds begin and end at this marker. Knit 7 rnds (hem) Change to #3 circular needle and purl one rnd. (Ridge formed for hem turning.) Knit 2 rnds each of the following colors: A, B, C, D, E.

Change to #4 circular needle and work the 25 rnds of CHART A, working the 30-st repeat 7–8–9–10 times around the body of the sweater.

Change to #3 needle and COLOR A. Knit until piece measures 11.5–12.5–13.5–14.5 inches from ridge in hem.

Divide for Armholes: Work 105–120–135–150 sts. Place a marker. Work to 6–6–6–8 sts before original marker. Cast off next 12–12–12–16 sts. Work to 6–6–6–8 sts before second marker. Cast off next 12–12–12–16 sts. Work to end of round. (93–108–123–134 sts each for front and back.

FRONT: Using a #3 straight needle, knit the 93–108–123–134 sts from circular needle. Slip the other 93–108–123–134 sts onto a holder for back. All rows are now worked back and forth on straight needles in stockinette stitch.

Work until 4.5–5–5–5.75 inches from armhole divide, ending with a purl row.

Shape Front Neck: Knit 38–44–51–55 sts, knit middle 17–20–21–24 sts and place on a holder for front neck, knit remaining 38–44–51–55 sts.

Right Shoulder: Purl one row. Beginning on next row, bind off 2 sts at neck edge every other row 3 times, then decrease 1 st at neck edge every 3–3–2–2 rows 7–8–10–10 times. Work 4–5–9–9 rows even. Place 25–30–35–39 sts on holder for shoulder.

Left Shoulder: Attach yarn at armhole edge. Knit one row. Work to correspond to right front.

BACK: Slip sts from holder or work off circular needle onto #3 straight needle. Attach yarn and work until 7.5–8.5–8.5–9.25 inches from armhole divide, ending with a purl row.

Shape Back Neck: Work 32–37–42–46 sts, work middle 29–34–39–42 sts and place on holder for back neck, work remaining 32–37–42–46 sts. Attach another ball of yarn for left side and working both sides at the same time, purl one row. Decrease 1 st at neck edge every row 7 times. Place remaining 25–30–35–39 sts onto holders for shoulders.

JOIN SHOULDERS: Use knitted seam method.

NECK: Using COLOR E and 16-inch circular #4 needle, starting at right shoulder seam pick up and knit 9 sts down right back, knit 29–34–39–42 sts from back neck holder, pick up and knit 9 sts up left back to shoulder seam, pick up and knit 25–27–27–27 sts down left front, knit 17–20–21–24 sts from front neck holder, pick up and knit 25–27–27–27 sts up right front to shoulder. (114–126–132–138 sts.) Work the first 7 rnds of CHART A, working the 6-st repeat 19–21–22–23 times around the neck. Change to #2 double-pointed or 16-inch circular. Work in K1, P1 ribbing for 2 rnds each of the following colors: E, D, C, B, A.

Work 4 rnds of knit in COLOR A. Bind off loosely in knit.

SLEEVES: With #2 double-pointed needles and COLOR A, cast on 44–46–52–56 sts. Join and place a marker. All rnds begin and end at this marker.

Work in K1, P1 ribbing for 3 rnds each of colors A, B, C, D, E, increasing 13–15–17–19 sts evenly spaced on the last rnd. (57–61–69–75 sts.)

Change to #4 needles and work the 25 rnds of CHART B, then change to #3 needles and COLOR A for remainder of sleeve.

Sleeve Increases: Increase 1 st at beginning and end of every 6–6–7–7 rnds 16–22–20–21 times, then every seventh rnd 3–0–0–0 times. (95–105–109–117 sts.)

Work 7–0–0–1 rnd(s) even. (124–132–140–148 rnds total).

Next rnd: Work to 13–13–13–15 sts before end of rnd. Cast off these 13–13–13–15 sts.

Next rnd: Cast off the first 13–13–13–15 sts, work to end of rnd.

Working back and forth on double-pointed needles, cast off 10 sts at the beginning of the next 6 rows. Cast off remaining 9–19–23–27 sts.

FINISHING: Set in sleeves, matching underarm increase line to middle of underarm cast-off on body. Turn hem under at ridge line and slip stitch in place. Steam lightly.

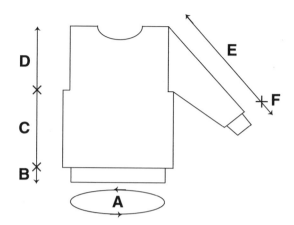

MEASUREMENTS (in inches)
A. 37–42–47–52
B. no ribbing
C. 11.5–12.5–13.5–14.5
D. 8.5–9.5–9.5–10.25
E. 16.5–17.5–18.5–19.5
F. 1.5

CHART A: BODY

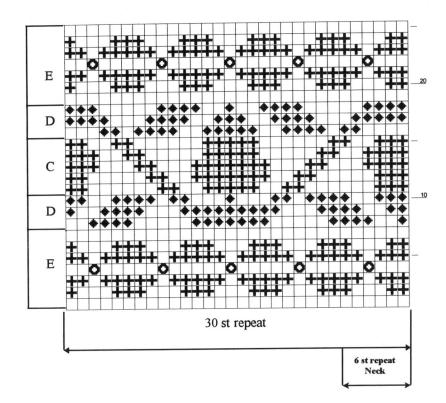

30 st repeat

6 st repeat
Neck

KEY FOR CHARTS

	background color, as indicated
◆	A. Bottle Green Tweed
✚	B. Aubergine
◉	F. Cornsilk

CHART B: SLEEVE

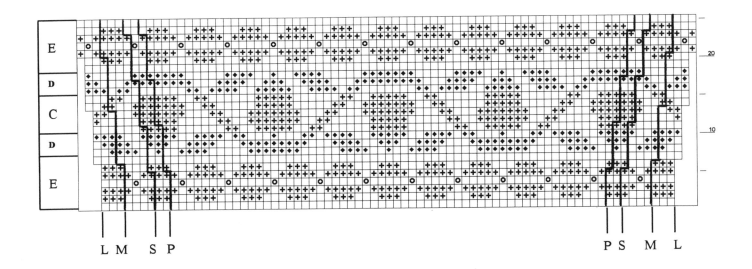

L M   S P   P S   M   L

◼ MEDALLION VEST

This vest is worked in subdued tones of the desert. The ridges add interest and texture. The entire vest is knit in the round, with steeks for the armholes, V-neck, and back neck. All directions for steeking are included in these instructions. For a general explanation of steeking, see the "Tips and Techniques" chapter. (Pictured on page 12.)

YARN: Harrisville Shetland Style (50 gm/1.75 oz skeins)

COLOR	SMALL	MED.	LARGE
A. Burgundy Tweed	2	2	3
B. Black	2	2	3
C. Camel	2	2	3
D. Sand	1	1	2
E. Lichen	1	2	2

NEEDLES: Circular #2 and #3 (24-inch and 16-inch)

GAUGE: 26 sts and 31 rows = 4 inches (worked over pattern on #3 needle).

FINISHED CHEST SIZES (in inches)

Small	39
Medium	43
Large	47.5

(For information on converting measurements and needle sizes to metric equivalents, see page 33.)

PATTERNS

Stockinette stitch: Knit every round.
K1, P1 ribbing.
Ridge: Knit 1 round, purl 1 round.

BODY: With #2 circular needle (24-inch) and COLOR E, cast on 222–250–278 sts. Join and place a marker. All rnds begin and end at this marker.

Work in K1, P1 ribbing for 2 rnds each in the following color sequence: E, B, C, D, A, D, C, B, E. (18 rnds total.) Knit one rnd in COLOR E, increasing 30 sts evenly spaced. (252–280–308 sts.)

Change to #3 (24-inch) circular needle and begin work from CHART A. Beginning on rnd 15–1–15, work the 14-st repeat for your size 18–20–22 times around the body of the vest. *For size Small:* work rnds 15–42 three times. *For Medium:* work

rnds 1–14, then work rnds 15–42 three times. *For Large:* work rnds 15–42 four times. Then *for all sizes,* work rnds 15–34. (104–118–132 rnds.)

On rnd 35, work 126–140–154 sts, place a marker, work to end of rnd. This divides your work into front and back.

DIVIDE FOR ARMHOLES AND FRONT NECK: On the next rnd you will be casting on your steek stitches. These 10 extra stitches form a bridge where the armhole and neck openings will be, and allow work to continue in the round. Later on, these steek stitches will be cut up the middle to form the armhole and neck openings, trimmed, and hemmed down. The stitches for the neck and armband ribbing will be picked up around these openings.

Following rnd 36 of Chart A, work 63–70–77 sts, place next stitch (middle stitch of front) on a pin, place a marker, cast on 10 steek sts in alternating colors, place a marker. This is your front neck steek. *Work to 8–9–10 sts before next marker, place next 17–19–21 sts on a pin, place a marker, cast on 10 steek sts in alternating colors, place a marker*. Repeat between *s. These are your armhole steeks. (109–121–133 sts for back; 54–60–66 sts on either side of front neck steek.)

(Continue working the steek stitches in alternating colors on subsequent rnds, reversing the order on each rnd. *Remember to work the steek stitches in knit, even on the ridge rows that call for purl.* Ends do not need to be worked in anymore, since the steek will be cut and the ends trimmed away. All rnds now begin and end at stitch #5 of the first armhole steek. This is where all new colors will be joined in.)

Work 1 rnd of CHART B.

ARMHOLE AND NECK SHAPING: The armhole and neck shaping is done simultaneously on either side of the 3 steeks. Decreases are worked as follows. This example describes a rnd with decreases at armholes *and* neck.

(Begin sample rnd: K first 5 steek sts, K2 together, work to 2 sts before front neck steek, K2 together, knit the 10 neck steek stitches, SSK, work to 2 sts before armhole steek, SSK, knit the 10 armhole steek stitches, K2 together, work all stitches of back to 2 sts before next armhole steek, SSK, knit last 5 armhole steek sts. End of sample rnd.)

Note: Even though a decrease may fall on a purl round of the ridge pattern, always work the 2 decrease sts knitwise.

Beginning on rnd 2 of Chart B, decrease 1 st each side of armholes every rnd 8–9–10 times, then every other rnd 9 times. (75–85–95 sts for back). *At the same time,* decrease 1 st each side of front neck steek on rnd 2, then every third rnd 22 times, then every fourth rnd 0–0–3 times. (14–19–21 sts for each front shoulder.) Back neck shaping begins 6 rnds before end.

BACK NECK SHAPING: On rnd 64–64–78, work 17–22–24 sts of back, place middle 41–41–47 sts on a holder for back neck, place a marker, cast on 10 steek sts in alternating colors, place a marker, work remaining 17–22–24 sts of back. Beginning on next rnd decrease 1 st each side of back neck steek 3 times. (14–19–21 sts for each shoulder). Back neck decreases are worked the same as front neck decreases. Back neck steek is worked the same as armhole and front neck steeks.

LAST RND: On rnd 69–69–83, cast off first 5 steek sts, work to front steek, cast off the 10 steek sts, work to armhole steek, cast off these 10 steek sts, work to back neck steek, cast off these 10 steek sts, work to next armhole steek, cast off the last 5 steek sts.

CUTTING THE STEEKS: Using the zigzag stitch on a sewing machine, or backstitching by hand, sew through the cast-on and cast-off edges of all steeks. Using a sharp pair of scissors, cut up the middle of the steeks between sts #5 and #6.

While most directions call for trimming them down to a 2-stitch width, I prefer the security of keeping them at 5 stitches. Turn back the 5 steek sts, hemming them down by hand using an overcast stitch and a strand of yarn. Be careful that your stitching does not show through on the right side. When you have finished, work back over the stitches in the opposite direction, forming Xs.

Steam gently.

JOIN SHOULDERS: Use the knitted seam method, but hold shoulders wrong sides together. (For this vest, the shoulder seam *should* form a slight ridge.) Use COLOR B–B–A.

NECKBAND: With right side facing, beginning at right shoulder seam and using #2 needle (16-inch) with COLOR E, pick up and knit 7 sts down right back, knit the 41–41–47 sts from back neck holder decreasing 1 st at center back, pick up and knit 7 sts up left back to shoulder seam, pick up and knit 68–68–82 sts down left front to center pin, place a marker, knit st from pin, place a marker, pick up and knit 68–68–82 sts up right front, place a marker. (191–191–225 sts.)

Work in K1, P1 ribbing in the following color/rnd sequence, working center front decreases on every rnd.

Color/Rnd. Sequence: 1 rnd COLOR E, 2 rnds each COLORS B, C, A, then 1 rnd COLOR E. (8 rnds total.)

Center front decrease: Work to 2 sts before center front stitch, K2 together through the *backs* of loops, slip marker, knit center front stitch, K2 together through *fronts* of loops, work to end of rnd.

Cast off in knit using COLOR E, working the center front decrease.

ARMBANDS: With #2 (16-inch) needle and COLOR E, knit the last 9–10–11 sts from underarm pin. Pick up and knit 69–69–83 sts to shoulder seam, pick up and knit 68–68–82 sts to underarm pin, knit last 8–9–10 sts from pin. Place a marker. (154–156–186 sts.) Work in K1, P1 ribbing in the same color/rnd sequence as neck. Bind off in knit using COLOR E.

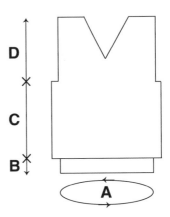

MEASUREMENTS (in inches)
  A. 39–43–47.5
  B. 2
  C. 13.5–15.5–17.25
  D. 9–9–11

KEY FOR CHARTS

- A. Black
- B. Burgundy
- Black ridge
- Burgundy ridge
- background color

CHART A: BODY
(Pattern Repeat)

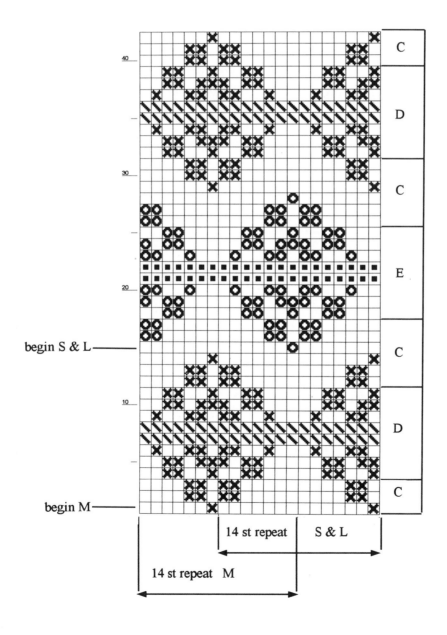

CHART B: ARMHOLE AND NECK SHAPING

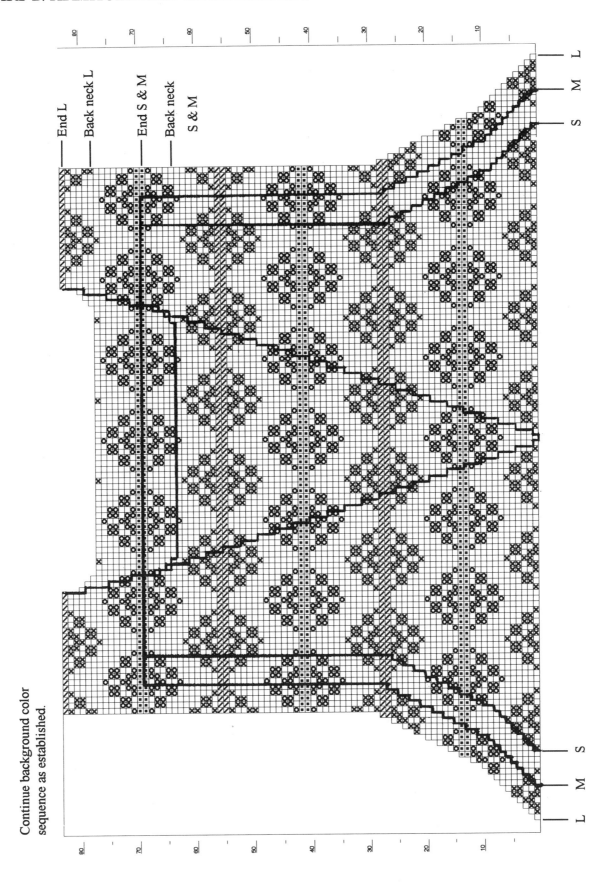

✠ PERSIAN FAIR ISLE

The colors in this sweater remind me of a Persian rug. This Fair Isle sweater is worked entirely in the round, with steeks for the armholes, front neck, and back neck. All directions for steeking are included in these instructions. For a general explanation of steeking, see the "Tips and Techniques" chapter. (Pictured on page 12.)

YARN: Harrisville Shetland style (50 gm/1.75 oz skeins)

COLOR	SMALL	LARGE
A. Topaz	1	2
B. Russet	3	5
C. Loden Blue	2	4
D. Black	2	4
E. Suede	2	4
F. Lichen	2	4
G. Camel	2	5
H. Sand	1	2
I. Gold	1	1

NEEDLES: #3 circular (24-inch and 16-inch), double-pointed #3.

GAUGE: 27 sts and 31 rows = 4 inches (worked over pattern on #3 needle).

FINISHED CHEST SIZES: Small 41.5 inches; Large 50 inches.

(For information on converting measurements and needle sizes to metric equivalents, see page 33.)

PATTERN: Stockinette Stitch (knit every round).

BODY: With #3 circular needle (24-inch) and COLOR B, cast on 280–336 sts. Join and place a marker. All rnds begin and end at this marker. Work in K2, P2 ribbing for 3 inches.

Change to CHART A, working the 28-st repeat indicated for your size 10–12 times around the body of the sweater. Work the 40 rnds of the chart 3–4 times. (120–160 rnds total.)

On the last rnd of the last chart repeat, work 140–168 sts, place a marker, work to end of rnd. This divides your work into front and back.

DIVIDE FOR ARMHOLES AND BEGIN STEEKS: On the next rnd you will be casting on your steek stitches. These 10 extra stitches form a

bridge where the armhole openings will be, and allow work to continue in the round. Later on, these steek stitches will be cut up the middle to form the armhole opening, trimmed, and hemmed down. The sleeve stitches will be picked up around this opening.

Following rnd 1 of CHART A and beginning at marker *work to 6 sts before next marker, place the next 13 sts on a pin*, place a marker, cast on 10 steek sts, alternating colors, place a marker, repeat between *s, place a marker, cast on 5 sts in alternating colors, change to colors used in rnd 2 of CHART B, cast on 5 sts in alternating colors, place a marker. You will now be working on 127–155 sts each for the front and back.

(Continue working the steek stitches in alternating colors on on subsequent rnds, reversing the order on each rnd. Ends do not need to be worked in anymore, since the steek will be cut and the ends trimmed away. All rnds begin and end at st #5 of the steek. This is where all new colors will be joined in.)

Work rnds 2 through 40 of CHART B, then repeat rnds 1 through 7 again. *Remember:* Begin at line indicated for your size, work to end of the repeat for your size, then work the entire 28-st repeat. Front and back are worked the same.

SHAPE NECK: Following rnd 1 of CHART C, work 44–58 sts, put middle 39 sts on a holder for front neck, place a marker, cast on 10 sts for front neck steek, alternating colors, place a marker, work remaining 44–58 sts of front. Work the 127–155 sts of back. This front neck steek is worked exactly the same as the armhole steeks.

Continue working the armhole steeks and the front neck steek. The back is worked straight until shortly before the end. You will begin shaping the back neck while you are still shaping the front neck.

FRONT: Decrease 1 st each side of neck every rnd 5 times. Work 1 rnd Beginning on the next rnd decrease 1 st at each side of neck every third rnd 6 times. Decreases are worked as follows: Work to 2 sts before front steek, K2 tog, knit steek sts, SSK. Work 2 rnds.

At the same time, begin back neck shaping where indicated on the chart.

Last Rnd of Front: Following rnd 26, cast off 5 steek sts at armhole at beginning of rnd, work sts of front, casting off 10 front neck steek sts, cast off 10 armhole steek sts, work remaining sts, cast off remaining 5 steek sts of armhole. Place 33–47 sts on holders for shoulders.

BACK. *Note:* Back is worked 1 more rnd than front. On the nineteenth rnd of Chart C, work 40–54 sts of back, place middle 47 sts on a holder for back neck, place a marker, cast on 10 steek sts alternating colors, place a marker, work remaining 40–54 sts of back. This back steek is worked the same as armhole and front neck steeks. Work 1 rnd, then decrease 1 st each side of neck every rnd 6 times.

Last Rnd and Decrease: Rnd. 27 Attach yarn to right armhole. Work to 2 sts before steek, K2 together, bind off 9 steek sts, K2 together, pass first stitch over the K2 together as in a standard cast-off, work to end. Place 33–47 sts on holders for shoulders.

CUTTING THE STEEKS: Using a zigzag stitch on a sewing machine or backstitching by hand, sew through the cast-on and cast-off edges of all steeks. Using a sharp pair of scissors, cut up the middle of the steeks between sts 5 and 6. Trim away ends left from changing colors.

While most directions for steeking call for trimming them down to a 2 stitch width, I prefer the security of keeping them at 5 stitches. Turn back the 5 steek sts, hemming them down by hand using an overcast stitch. Be careful that your stitching does not show through on the right side. When you have finished, work back over the stitches in the opposite direction, forming Xs.

Steam gently.

JOIN SHOULDERS: Use the knitted seam method.

NECK. *Note:* When picking up stitches around openings that have been steeked, use the stitch directly adjacent to the last steek stitch. Insert the needle through both loops of the stitch, draw yarn through, and knit.

With right side facing and starting at left shoulder seam, using #3 (16-inch) circular needle and COLOR B, pick up and knit 28 sts down left front, knit 39 sts from front neck holder, pick up and knit 28 sts up right front neck to shoulder seam, pick up and knit 10 sts down right back, knit the 47 sts from back neck holder, pick up and knit 10 sts up left back. (162 sts.) Work one rnd in purl. Work CHART D, beginning where indicated, then working the 18-st repeat 8 times, then working the first 6 sts of the repeat.

Knit one rnd, decreasing 22 sts on the last rnd (K7, K2 tog, *K5, K2 together* repeat between *s 21 times, end K6) 140 sts. Work in K2, P2 ribbing for 1.5 inches. Bind off in rib.

SLEEVES: With 16-inch #3 needle and COLOR F, knit last 6 sts from underarm pin, pick up and knit 75 sts to shoulder seam, pick up and knit another 75 sts to underarm pin, knit 6 sts from pin, place a marker, knit last st, place a marker. (163 sts.) The stitch between the markers is the underarm st, and is always knit in background color. All decreasing is done on either side of this st as follows: K2 together at beginning of rnd, work to 2 sts before marker, SSK, knit underarm st.

To Read Chart E: Work begins on rnd 6 on fourth stitch from right side of chart. Vertical lines show the decreases. Begin at vertical line #1, work to end of stitch repeat, then work full 28-st repeat. Work the vertical lines in numerical order. *Remember: Decreases are only shown for beginning of rnd. Do not foget to work them also at end of rnd.*

Following SLEEVE CHART, work 3 rnds, then decrease 1 st at beginning and end of every third rnd 37–40 times.(89–83 sts.) Change to double-pointed needles when necessary. Work 4–15 rnds even, ending on rnd 1–21. Work 1 rnd in COLOR B, decreasing 41–29 sts evenly spaced. (48–54 sts.) Continue in Color B, working K2, P2 ribbing for 3 inches. Bind off in rib.

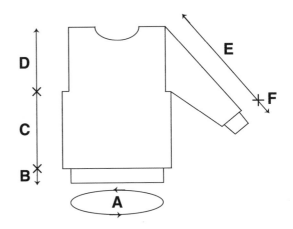

MEASUREMENTS (in inches)

A. 41.5–50
B. 3
C. 15.5–10.5
D. 9.25
E. 14.75–17.5
F. 3

CHART A:
BODY

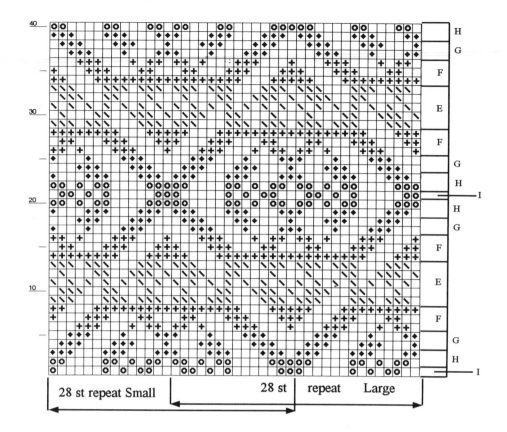

CHART B:
ARMHOLES

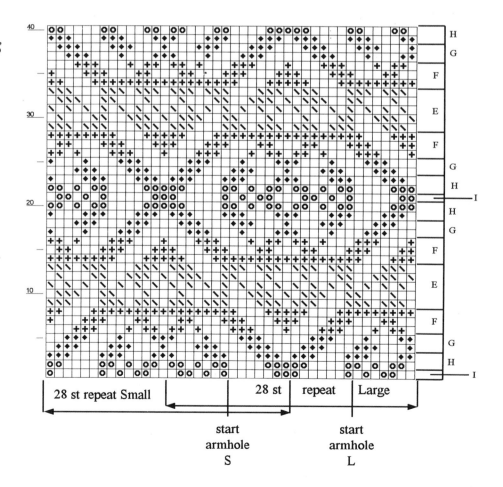

CHART C: NECK SHAPING

KEY FOR CHARTS

- A. Topaz
- B. Russet
- C. Loden Blue
- D. Black
- background color

CHART D: NECK
Background—Knit
Pattern—Purl

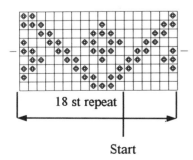

18 st repeat

Start

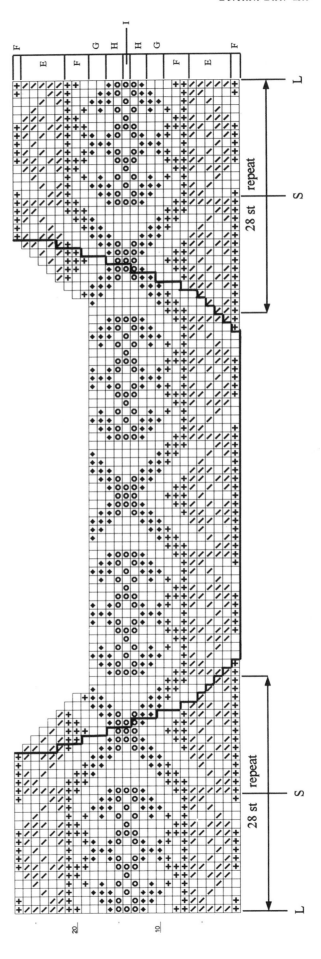

CHART E: SLEEVE

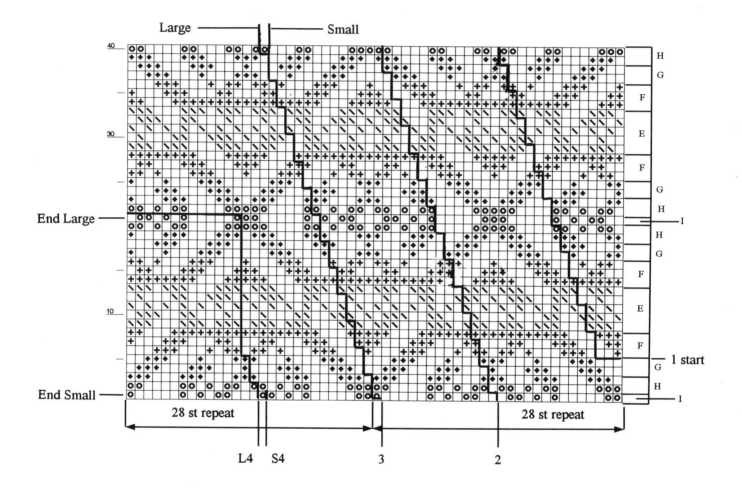

FAIR ISLE IN NATURAL SHADES

This pullover is worked entirely in the round, with steeks for the armholes, front neck, and back neck. It uses traditional Fair Isle ribbing: K2 in one color, P2 in another color. All directions for steeking are included in these instructions. For a general explanation of steeking, see the "Tips and Techniques" chapter. (Pictured on page 18.)

YARN: Harrisville Shetland style (50 gm/1.75 oz skeins)

COLOR	SMALL	LARGE
A. Loden Blue	1	1
B. Russet	1	1
C. Black	1	2
D. Cocoa	2	3
E. Teak	1	1
F. Topaz	1	1
G. Driftwood	1	2
H. Camel	1	1
I. Sand	2	2
J. Suede	2	2
K. Sandalwood	1	1
L. Oatmeal	1	2
M. White	1	1

NEEDLES: Circular #2 and #3 (24-inch), circular #2 and #3 (16-inch), double-pointed #2 and #3.

GAUGE: 27 sts and 28 rows = 4 inches (worked over pattern on #3 needle).

FINISHED CHEST SIZES (in inches)

Small	41
Large	51

(For information on converting measurements and needle sizes to metric equivalents, see page 33.)

PATTERNS
Corrugated rib: K2 in one color, P2 in other color
Stockinette Stitch: K every round

A Note on Carrying Yarn: This design has three rnds that use only one color between each band of pattern. Because gauge can change significantly when using one color as opposed to two, I suggest that a second color be carried and woven in around these one-color rounds. This will ensure even tension throughout the sweater. Use the color that was previously employed, or change to the color that will be used next in the chart. Carry all yarn not in use loosely, spreading stitches to their true width on the needle. Weave in yarn every 3 or 4 stitches.

BODY: With #2 circular needle (24-inch) and COLOR C, cast on 260–324 sts. Place a marker and join. All rnds begin and end at this marker. Work in corrugated rib for 28–33 rnds as follows.

Work sequences I and II, then sequence I in reverse order.

Sequence I	COLORS K2	P2	# OF RNDS SMALL	LARGE
	C	G	1	2
	A	G	2	2
	D	H	2	3
	D	I	1	1
	F	I	1	1
	C	J	1	1
	D	J	1	1
	D	K	2	2
	E	L	2	2
Sequence II	COLORS K2	P2	# OF RNDS SMALL	LARGE
	B	M	2	3

Change to #3 needle. Knit one rnd in COLOR C, increasing 28–36 sts evenly spaced. (288–360 sts.) Begin working where indicated for your size (Rnd. 23–1) from CHART A, working the 36-st repeat for your size 8–10 times around body of sweater. *For size Small,* work to end of chart, then repeat the entire 48 rnds of chart 1 more time. *For size Large,* work the 48 rnds of chart 2 complete times. (74–96 rnds.) *For both sizes:* On the last round of the last repeat of the chart, work 144–180 sts, place a marker, work to end of rnd. This divides your work into front and back.

Size Small only, work CHART B through rnd 9.

DIVIDE FOR ARMHOLES AND BEGIN STEEKS:
On the next rnd you will be casting on your steek stitches. These 10 extra stitches form a bridge where the armhole openings will be, and al-

low work to continue in the round. Later on, these steek stitches will be cut up the middle to form the armhole opening, trimmed, and hemmed down. The sleeve stitches will be picked up around this opening.

Following CHART B, rnd 10–1, beginning at first marker, *work to 4 sts before marker, put next 7 sts onto a pin*, place a marker, cast on 10 steek stitches in alternating colors, place a maker, * repeat between *s, place a marker, cast on 5 steek sts in alternating colors, change to colors used in rnd 11–2 of Chart B, cast on 5 steek sts in alternating colors, place a marker.

Ends do not need to be worked in anymore, since the steek will be cut and the ends trimmed away. All rnds begin and end at st #5 of the steek. This is where all new colors will be joined in. Work all steeks in alternating colors, reversing the order on each rnd.

Work 1 rnd, then decrease 1 st each side of each armhole 5 times. (127–163 sts each for front and back.) Decreases are worked as follows: Work 5 steek sts, slip marker, K2 tog, work sts of front to 2 sts before armhole marker, SSK, slip marker and work 10 steek sts, slip marker, K2 tog., work sts of back until 2 sts before next armhole, SSK, slip marker, work 5 steek sts. End of rnd.

Work through rnd 54 of Chart B. *Note: On chart, decreases are shown only for beginning of armhole. Do not forget to work decreases on the other side as well.* Decreasing is done 4 times in each rnd.

SHAPE NECK: Begin working CHART C, following established pattern repeats. *Note: Chart shows only center portion of sweater.*

Following rnd 1 of Chart C, work 52–70 sts of front, place next 23 sts onto a holder for front neck, place a marker, cast on 10 steek sts for front neck, alternating colors, place a marker, work to end of rnd. This front neck steek is worked exactly the same as the armhole steeks.

Continue working the armhole steeks and the front neck steek. The back is worked straight until shortly before the end. You will begin shaping the back neck while you are still shaping the front neck.

Front Neck: Decrease 1 st each side of front neck 7–7 times, then every other rnd. 10–10 times. Decreases are worked as follows before and after neck steek: K2 together, work 10 steek sts, SSK.

Back Neck: On rnd 22, work 41–59 sts of back, place next 45 sts onto a holder for back neck, place a marker, cast on 10 steek sts alternating colors, place a marker, work to end of rnd. This back steek

is worked the same as armhole and front neck steek. Beginning on next rnd, decrease 1 st each side of back neck 5 times. (Decreases are worked the same as for front neck.) The sixth decrease rnd is worked as follows:

Last Back Neck Decrease (Rnd. 28): Work first 5 steek sts at beginning of rnd, work all sts of front (working decreases as indicated) to second armhole steek stitches, cast off these 10 steek sts, work to 2 sts before back neck steek, K2 together, cast off 9 steek sts, K2 together, cast off last steek st by passing it over this K2 together stitch, work remaining sts of back, cast off 10 armhole steek sts.

Rnd 29: Work last row of front, casting off front neck steek sts. *Note: Front is worked one row more than back.*

Put remaining 35–53 sts onto #3 double-pointed needles for shoulders.

CUTTING THE STEEKS: Using the zigzag stitch on a sewing machine, or backstitching by hand, sew through all cast-on and cast-off edges of all steeks. Using a sharp pair of scissors, cut up the middle of the steeks between sts 5 and 6. Trim away ends left from changing colors.

While most directions for steeking call for trimming them down to a 2-stitch width, I prefer the security of keeping them at 5 stitches. Turn back the 5 steek sts, hemming them down by hand using an overcast stitch. Be careful that your stitching does not show through on the right side. When you have finished, work back over the stitches in the opposite direction, forming Xs.

Steam gently.

JOIN SHOULDERS: Use the knitted seam method.

NECK. *Note:* When picking up stitches around openings that have been steeked, use the stitch directly adjacent to the last steek stitch. Insert the needle through both loops of the stitch, draw yarn through, and knit.

With right side facing and starting at right shoulder seam, using COLOR C and #2 circular needle (16-inch), pick up and knit 9 sts along back right neck, knit the 45 sts from back neck holder, pick up and knit 9 sts along left back neck to shoulder, pick up and knit 29 sts along left front, knit the 23 sts from front neck holder, pick up and knit 29 sts along right front to shoulder seam. (144 sts.)

Work in corrugated rib in the following color/rnd sequence (11–14 rnds). Work sequences I and II, then sequence I in reverse order.

	COLORS		# OF RNDS	
	K2	P2	SMALL	LARGE
Sequence I	C	G	1	1
	A	G	1	2
	D	K	2	2
	F	I	1	1
Sequence II	B	M	1	2

Cast off in knit using COLOR C.

SLEEVES: With #3 circular needle (16-inch) and COLOR C, knit the last 3 sts from pin, pick up and knit 73–83 sts to shoulder seam, pick up and knit 73–83 sts to pin, knit 3 sts from pin, place a marker, knit last st from pin, place a marker. (153–173 sts.)

The stitch between the markers is the underarm st, and is always knit in background color. All decreasing is done on either side of this st as follows: Beginning of rnd: K2 together, work to 2 sts before marker, SSK, knit underarm stitch.

To Read Chart D or E: Work begins on rnd 43 at first st at upper right side of chart. Work to left side of chart, then work the 36 st repeat to end of rnd. After working the topmost line of the chart, move down to the bottom line, starting that rnd at vertical decrease line #2. On the last pass up the chart, commence at vertical line #3. *Remember: Decrease lines on sleeve chart are shown only for the beginning of the rnd. Do not forget to work decreases at the end of the rnd also.*

Following CHART D or E for your size, beginning on rnd 43, work 1 rnd.

Beginning on next rnd, decrease 1 st at beginning and end of every other rnd 10 times, then every 3rd. rnd 27–30 times. (79–93 sts.) Work even for 0–13 rnds, ending with a completed rnd 47–21.

Knit 1 rnd in COLOR C, decreasing 11–17 sts evenly spaced. (68–76 sts.)

Change to #2 double-pointed needles and work in ribbing as for body for your size. Bind off in Color C in rib.

FINISHING: Weave in any loose ends. Steam lightly.

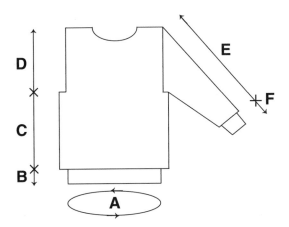

MEASUREMENTS (in inches)
A. 41–51
B. 3.5–4
C. 10.5–13.5
D. 10.5–11.5
E. 14.5–17.5
F. 3.5–4

CHART A:
BODY

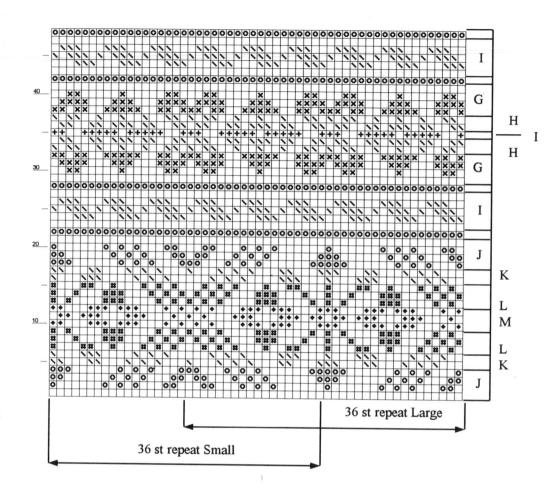

36 st repeat Large

36 st repeat Small

KEY FOR CHARTS

⊠	A. Loden blue
◆	B. Russet
◉	C. Black
╲	D. Cocoa
✿	E. Teak
✛	F. Topaz
☐	background color, as indicated

CHART C: NECK
(Left Side)

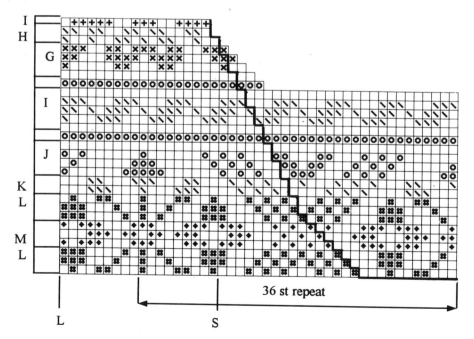

36 st repeat

CHART B:
ARMHOLES

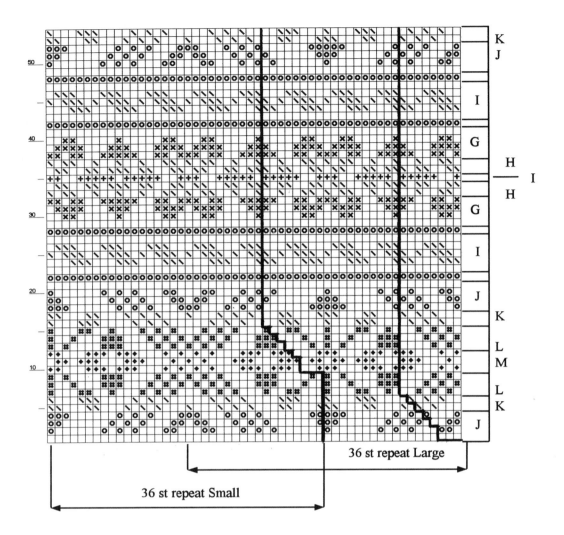

36 st repeat Large

36 st repeat Small

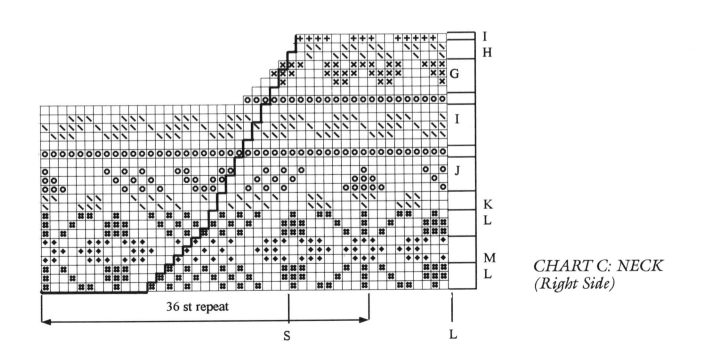

36 st repeat

S

L

CHART C: NECK
(Right Side)

CHART D: SLEEVE
(Small)

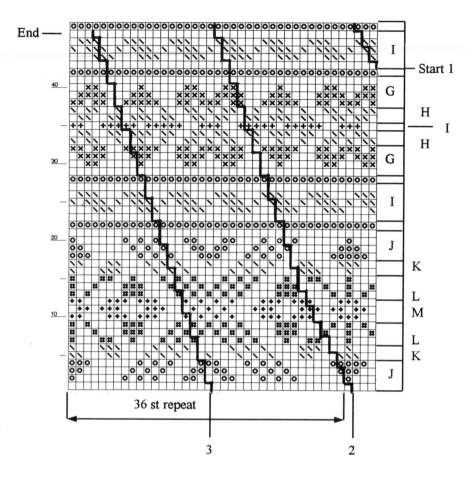

CHART D: SLEEVE
(Large)

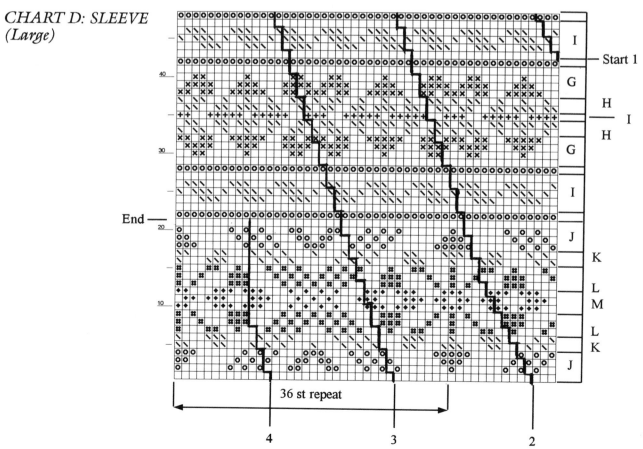

FAIR ISLE SCROLL

The graceful curves of this design reminded me of the beautiful scroll on my French cello. Using 10 colors, the design harmoniously blends rosy purples and subtle grays. Traditional corrugated ribbing is worked in a color combination that produces a checkered look. Worked entirely in the round, this sweater uses steeks for the armholes and neck. All directions for steeking are included in these instructions. For a general explanation of steeking, see the "Tips and Techniques" chapter. (Pictured on page 16.)

YARN: Harrisville Shetland style (50 gm/1.75 oz skeins)

COLOR	SKEINS
A. Garnet	2
B. Blackberry	2
C. Pewter	2
D. Woodsmoke	1
E. Aster	1
F. Apple Blossom	1
G. Pearl	1
H. Silver Mauve	1
I. Aubergine	2
J. Purple Haze	2

NEEDLES: #3 circular (32 inch and 16 inch), #3 double-pointed needles

GAUGE: 27 sts and 31 rows = 4 inches (worked over pattern on #3 needle).

FINISHED CHEST SIZE: 47.5 inches

(For information on converting measurements and needle sizes to metric equivalents, see page 33.)

PATTERNS

Stockinette Stitch: Knit every round.

Corrugated Rib: K2 in one color, P2 in other color.

BODY: With 32 inch circular needle and COLOR I, cast on 320 sts. Place a marker and join. All rnds begin and end at this marker.

Work in corrugated rib for 20 rnds, working 2 rnds each in the following color sequence:

KNIT 2	PURL 2
I	G
G	I

A	C
C	A
D	F
F	D
B	E
E	B
J	H
H	J

Knit 1 rnd in COLOR J.

Work the 24 rnds of CHART A 4 times, working the 32-st repeat 10 times around the body of the sweater. Then work rnds 1–11. On rnd 12, work 160 sts, place a marker, work remaining 160 sts. This divides your work into front and back.

DIVIDE FOR ARMHOLES AND BEGIN STEEKS: On this rnd you will be casting on your steek stitches. These 10 extra stitches form a bridge where the armhole opening will be, and allow work to continue in the round. Later on, these steek stitches will be cut up the middle to form the armhole opening, trimmed, and hemmed down. The sleeve stitches will be picked up around this opening.

Following rnd 13 of Chart A, *work to 3 sts before next marker, slip next 7 sts onto a pin, * place a marker, cast on 10 steek stitches in alternating colors, place a marker, repeat between *s, place a marker, cast on 5 sts in alternating colors, change to colors used in rnd 14 of Chart A, cast on 5 sts using these colors, place a marker. Ends do not need to be worked in anymore, since the steek will be cut and the ends trimmed away. All rnds begin and end at st #5 of this steek. This is where all new colors will be joined in. Work all steeks in alternating colors, reversing the order on each rnd.

You are now working on 153 sts each for the front and back.

Following CHART B, work rnds 14–24, rnds 1–24, then rnds 1–13.

Change to CHART C and work rnd 1.

SHAPE NECK: On rnd 2, work 63 sts, place middle 27 sts on a holder for front neck, place a marker, cast on 10 steek sts in alternating colors, place a marker, work remaining 63 sts of front, work the 153 sts of back. This front neck steek is worked exactly the same as the armhole steeks. Continue working the armhole steeks and the front neck steek. The back is worked straight until shortly before the end. You will begin shaping the back neck while you are still shaping the front neck.

Front Neck: Decrease 1 st each side of front neck every rnd 7 times, then every other rnd 3 times, then every 3rd rnd 2 times. Decreases are worked as follows: Work to 2 sts before neck steek, K2 together, work 10 steek sts, SSK. Work 2 rnds even.

Back Neck: On rnd 17, work 57 sts, place middle 39 sts on holder for back neck, place a marker, cast on 10 steek sts in alternating colors, place a marker, work remaining 57 sts of back.

Decrease 1 st each side of back neck every rnd 5 times. Decreases are worked the same as front neck.

LAST RND FOR BACK (Rnd. 23): Work 5 steek sts, work all sts of front, cast off 10 armhole steek sts, work to 2 sts before back neck steek, K2 together, cast off 9 back neck steek sts, K2 together, cast off last steek st over this K2 together stitch. Work remaining back sts, cast off 5 armhole steek sts. Change colors for next rnd.

LAST RND FOR FRONT (Rnd 24). *Note:* Front is worked 1 more row than back. Cast off remaining 5 steek sts, work to front neck steek, cast off 10 front neck steek sts, work remaining sts of front.

Place 51 sts for each shoulder on a #3 double-pointed needle.

CUTTING THE STEEKS: Using the zigzag stitch on a sewing machine, or back stitching by hand, sew through all cast-on and cast-off edges of all steeks. Using a sharp pair of scissors, cut up the middle of the steeks between sts #5 and #6. Trim away any ends.

While most directions for steeking call for trimming them down to a 2-stitch width, I prefer the security of keeping them at 5 stitches. Turn back the 5 steek sts, hemming them down by hand using an overcast stitch. Be careful that your stitching does not show through on the right side. When you have finished, work back over the stitches in the opposite direction, forming Xs.

Steam gently.

JOIN SHOULDERS: Use the knitted seam method.

NECK. *Note:* To pick up sts around steek openings, use the stitch directly adjacent to the last steek stitch. Insert the needle through both loops of the stitch, draw yarn through, and knit.

With 16-inch circular needle and COLOR B, starting at right shoulder, pick up and knit 10 sts down right back neck, knit the 39 sts from back neck holder, pick up and knit 10 sts up left back neck, pick up and knit 23 sts down left front, knit the 27 sts from front neck holder, pick up and knit 23 sts up right front. (132 sts.)

Work in corrugated rib, working 2 rnds each of the following color sequence:

KNIT 2	PURL 2
E	B
B	E
F	D
D	F
G	I
I	G

Bind off loosely in knit using COLOR I.

SLEEVES. *To read sleeve chart:* Work begins on first st at right side of chart. Begin at vertical line #1, work to end of stitch repeat, then work full 32-st repeat. Work the vertical lines in numerical order.

Remember: Decreases are only shown for beginning of rnd. Do not forget to work decreases at end of rnd also.

With 16-inch circular needle and COLOR G, knit last 3 sts from pin, pick up and knit 72 sts to shoulder seam, pick up and knit another 72 sts to pin, knit 3 sts from pin, place a marker, knit remaining st from pin, place a marker. (151 sts.)

This last stitch is the underarm stitch, and is always knit in background color. All decreasing is done on either side of this stitch as follows: At beginning of rnd K2 together, work to 2 sts before marker, SSK, knit underarm st

Following CHART D, decrease 1 st at beginning of rnd and 1 st at end of every third rnd 40 times. (71 sts.)

Next rnd: With COLOR J, knit, decreasing 7 sts evenly spaced. (64 sts.)

Work in corrugated rib as for body, but working the color sequence in reverse.

Bind off loosely in knit using COLOR I.

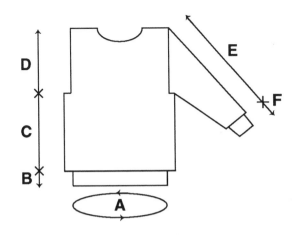

MEASUREMENTS (in inches)
A. 47.5   D. 9.5
B. 2.5   E. 15.5
C. 14   F. 2.5

KEY FOR CHARTS
- ✚ A. Garnet
- ⧄ B. Blackberry
- ◍ D. Woodsmoke
- ⊠ I. Aubergine
- ◆ J. Purple Haze
- ☐ background color, as indicated

CHART A:
LOWER BODY

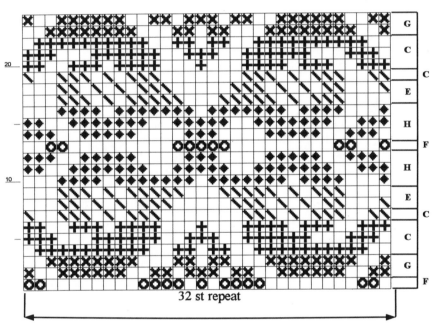

32 st repeat

CHART B:
UPPER BODY

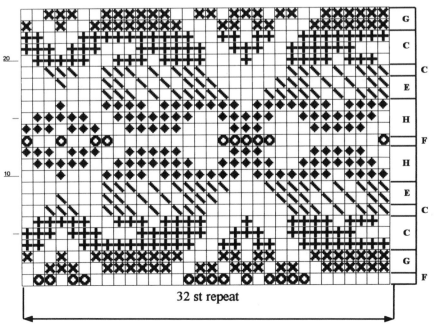

32 st repeat

CHART C: NECK SHAPING

CHART D: SLEEVE

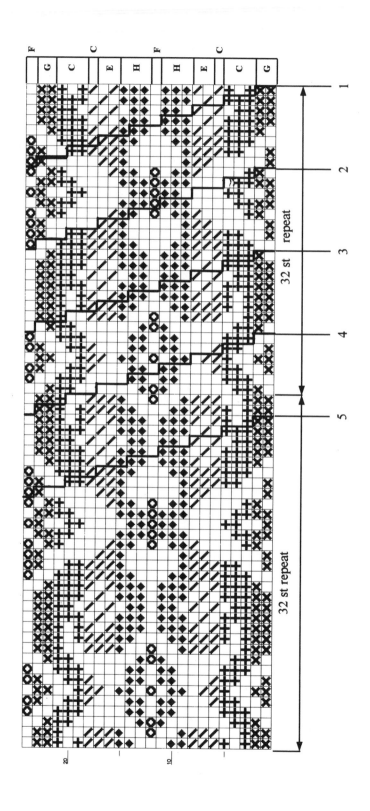

⊞ PURPLE TWEED WAISTCOAT

This vest is knit entirely in the round, with steeks for the center front and armholes. A very easy diamond pattern adds color and interest to the richness of the purple tweed. Corrugated rib completes the classic look. All directions for steeking are included in these instructions. For a general explanation of steeking, see the "Tips and Techniques" chapter. (Pictured on page 25.)

YARN: Harrisville Shetland Style (50 gm/1.75 oz skeins)

COLOR	SM., MED.	LGE., X-LGE.
A. Purple Tweed	3	4
B. Periwinkle	1	1
C. Lilac	1	1
D. Bermuda	1	1
E. Plum	1	1

NEEDLES: Circular #2 and #3 (24-inch and 16-inch)

GAUGE: 26 sts and 28 rows = 4 inches (worked over pattern on #3 needle).

FINISHED CHEST SIZES (in inches)

Small	37.5
Medium	39.5
Large	42
Extra Large	44.5

(For information on converting measurements and needle sizes to metric equivalents, see page 33.)

PATTERNS

Corrugated Rib: K2 in one color, P2 in another color.

Stockinette Stitch: Knit every round.

ACCESSORIES: 8 buttons (⅜-inch)

BODY: With 24-inch #3 circular needle and COLOR A, cast on 5 sts, place a marker, cast on 238–254–270–286 sts, place a marker, cast on 5 sts. The 10 sts between the markers are the front steek stitches. All rounds begin and end on stitch #5 of this steek. All new colors are joined here, but the ends do not need to be worked in since they will be trimmed away when the steek is cut up the middle to form the front opening. This steek will also be shaped, beginning at the armhole divide, for the V-neck.

To Work Steek: Knit every rnd, working each st in alternating colors on alternating rnds, but keeping first and last st in COLOR A for body of vest, and the color of K2 for the ribbing part. These first and last steek stitches that are worked in a constant color will be used when picking up stitches for the button and buttonhole band.

Join the round, and work in corrugated rib in the following color/rnd sequence, beginning and ending each rnd with a K2. Remember to work steek stitches in K only.

Work sequences I and II, then sequence I in reverse order, for a total of 27–27–27–27–31 rnds.

	COLORS		# OF RNDS.			
	K2	P2	SM.	MED.	LGE.	X-LGE.
Sequence I	A	B	4	4	4	5
	A	C	4	4	4	5
	E	C	4	4	4	4
Sequence II	A	D	3	3	3	3

Next rnd: With COLOR A, knit, increasing 3 sts evenly spaced. (241–257–273–289 sts.)

Following CHART A, work the 8-st repeat around the body of the vest 30–32–34–36 times, ending each rnd with the extra stitch indicated on the chart. Work the first 10 rnds of chart 7–7–8–8 times, then the next 5 rnds 0–1–0–1 time(s). (70–75–80–85 rnds.)

Work 0–5–10–15 rnds of CHART B.

DIVIDE FOR ARMHOLES AND SHAPE FRONT NECK: Beginning on rnd 1–6–11–16 of Chart B, work the first 5 steek sts, SSK for neck shaping, work *another* 51–54–57–60 sts. (52–55–58–61 sts on needle counting the 1 st left from the SSK), *place next 15–17–19–21 sts on a holder for underarm, place a marker, cast on 10 sts in alternating colors for armhole steek, place a marker.* Work 105–111–117–123 sts of back, work between *s, then work 51–54–57–60 sts, K2 together for neck shaping, knit last 5 front steek sts. End of rnd.

Continue decreasing in same manner for front

neck every other rnd 12–7–1–0 times, every third rnd 14–17–21–17 times, and every fourth rnd 0–0–0–3 times, and *at the same time* decrease 1 st *each side* of armhole steeks every rnd 7–8–9–10 times, then every other rnd 4 times. Armhole steeks are worked in the same manner as front steek, keeping the first and last st in Color A, and alternating colors and rnds for other 8 sts.

To Decrease: Two types of decrease are used; SSK slants to the left, K2 together slants to the right. The following diagram indicates which type of decrease to use where.

A. *SSK:* right front neck edge just after front steek

B. *SSK:* right front just before armhole steek

C. *K2 tog:* back just after armhole steek

D. *SSK:* back just before armhole steek

E. *K2 tog:* left front just after armhole steek

F. *K2 tog:* left front neck edge just before front steek.

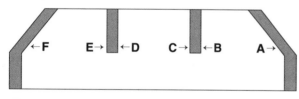

■ Steek stitches

After armhole shaping is completed, continue working straight at armholes, but still doing front neck decreasing. Change to 16-inch needle when necessary. Work through rnd 66–71–76–81.

Rnd. 67–72–77–82: Work any decreases still indicated on chart. Work 5 front steek sts, work right front, cast off the 10 sts of first armhole steek, work 15–19–23–27 sts and place on a holder for shoulder, work middle 53–49–45–41 sts and place on a holder for back neck, work remaining 15–19–23–27 sts and place on a holder for other shoulder, cast off 10 steek sts of other armhole steek, work left front, cast off last 5 front steek sts.

Last Rnd. (Rnd. 68–73–78–83): Cast off remaining 5 front steek sts, work right front and place these sts on a holder for shoulder. Attach yarns to left front at armhole edge and work last rnd. Place these sts on a holder for other shoulder. *Note:* Front is worked one row more than back. (15–19–23–27 sts on each holder for each shoulder)

CUTTING THE STEEKS: Using the zigzag stitch on a sewing machine, or backstitching by hand, sew through all cast-on and cast-off edges of all steeks. Using a sharp pair of scissors, cut up the middle of

the steeks between sts #5 and #6. Trim away ends.

While most directions for steeking call for trimming them down to a 2-stitch width, I prefer the security of keeping them at their full width. The first and last steek stitch that was always worked in COLOR A will *not* be turned under with the other steek stitches. Turn back the 4 alternating color steek sts, hemming them down by hand using an overcast stitch. Be careful that your stitching does not show through on the right side. When you have finished, work back over the stitches in the opposite direction, forming Xs.

Steam gently.

JOIN SHOULDERS: Use the knitted seam method.

FRONT BAND. *Note:* When picking up stitches around openings that have been steeked, use the steek stitch directly adjacent to the body of the garment. This is the stitch that was always worked in Color A (on ribbing it was worked in the K2 color). Insert the needle through both loops of the stitch, draw yarn through, and knit.

Mark the beginning of the front neck decreasing on both fronts with a safety pin. With #2 needle (24-inch) and COLOR A, starting at lower right front with right side facing, pick up and knit 27–27–27–31 sts along ribbing, pick up and knit 70–75–80–85 sts to beginning of front neck shaping (marked by the pin), place a marker on needle, pick up and knit 68 sts up right neck to shoulder seam (placing last st at shoulder seam), knit 53–49–45–41 sts from back neck holder decreasing 1 st for sizes Small and Large, and increasing 1 st for Medium and Extra Large. Pick up and knit 68 sts down left front to safety pin (placing first st on shoulder seam), pick up and knit 70–75–80–85 sts to beginning of ribbing, pick and knit 27–27–27–31 sts along ribbing. (382–390–394–410 sts.)

Work back and forth in P2, K2 ribbing in the color/row sequences below, making buttonholes on rows 4 and 5.

Wrong-side rows: *P2 in first color, K2* in second color, repeat between *s, end P2.

Right-side rows: *K2 in first color, P2* in second color, repeat between *s, end K2.

Beginning on a wrong-side row, work sequences I and II, then sequence I in reverse order.

	COLORS		# OF ROWS
Sequence I	A	B	1
	A	C	1
	E	C	1
Sequence II	A	D	2

To Make Buttonholes: Eight buttonholes are worked between bottom of vest and marker on needle. Row 4: Rib 2–4–3–4, cast off 2 sts, *rib 11–11–12–13 (this includes the st already left on the needle from the last cast-off), cast off 2 sts* repeat between *s 7 times, end rib 2–5–4–5. Slip marker and rib to end of row. Row 5: Rib, casting on 2 sts over each buttonhole.

Work to end of sequence. Bind off in purl using Color A.

ARMBANDS: With 16-inch #2 circular needle and COLOR A, knit the last 7–8–9–10 sts from holder, pick up and knit 67–68–69–70 sts to shoulder seam, pick up and knit 66–67–68–69 sts to underarm holder, knit remaining 8–9–10–11 sts from holder. Place a marker. (148–152–156–160 sts.) Work in ribbing the same color/rnd sequence as front band. Bind off in knit using Color A.

FINISHING: Sew on buttons. Weave in any loose ends. Steam gently.

KEY FOR CHARTS

☐	A. Purple Tweed
✿	B. Periwinkle
✚	C. Lilac
❖	D. Bermuda
◥	E. Plum

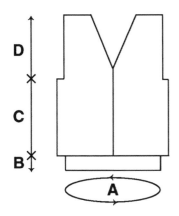

MEASUREMENTS (in inches)
A. 37.5–39.5–42–44.5
B. 3.5
C. 10–10.75–11.5–12.25
D. 9

CHART A: PATTERN REPEAT

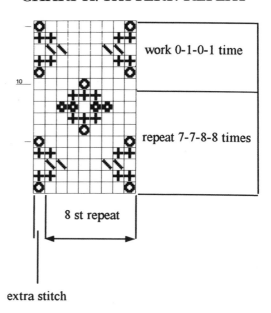

work 0-1-0-1 time

repeat 7-7-8-8 times

8 st repeat

extra stitch

CHART B: NECK & ARMHOLE SHAPING

Right Front

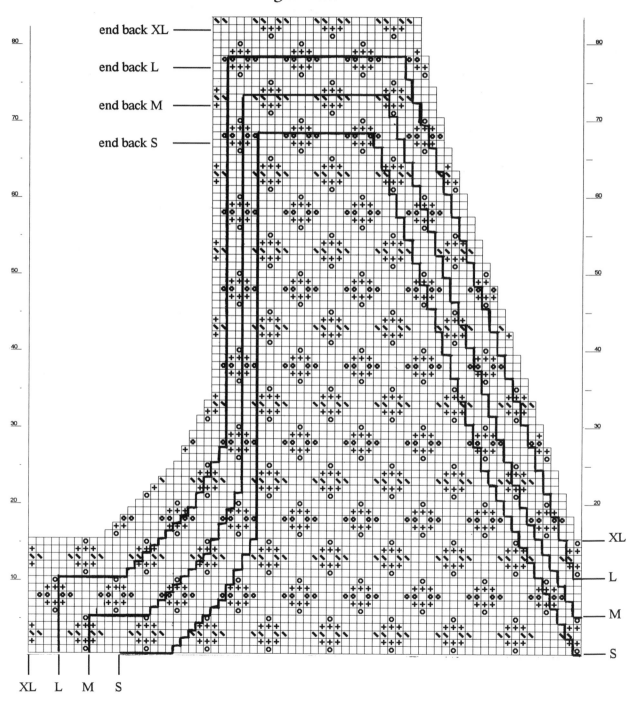

Left Front

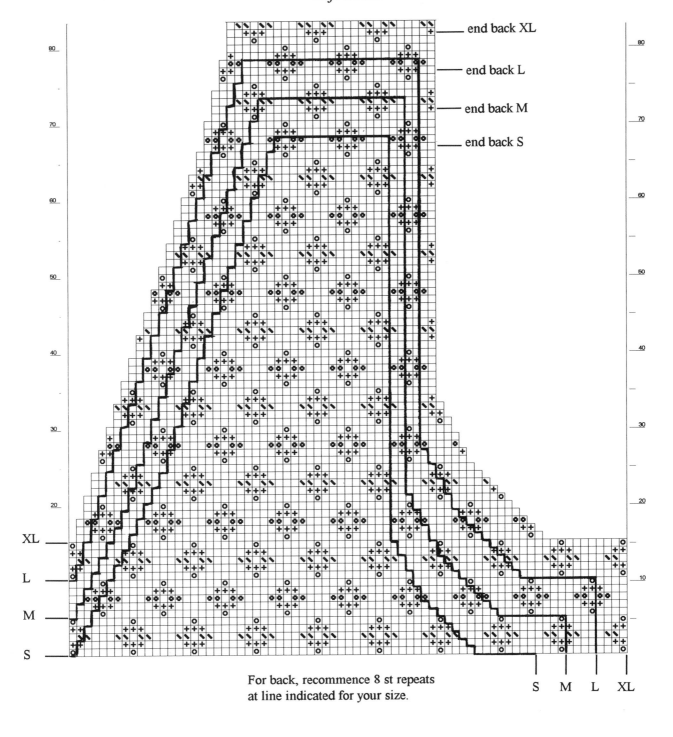

end back XL

end back L

end back M

end back S

For back, recommence 8 st repeats
at line indicated for your size.

S   M   L   XL

⊠ ENTRELAC SKI SOCKS

Because the entrelac technique produces a bias fabric, these socks stretch easily to fit over pants legs to help keep snow out. Although specific colors and amounts for yarn are given, it is the perfect project to use left-overs. Make sure to read the directions for knitting backward before starting, as it will save you from having to turn your work every six stitches! (Pictured on page 18.)

YARN: Harrisville Shetland Style (50 gm/1.75 oz skeins), one skein each of the following colors. (*Note:* Colors B through E require only about 15 grams, or 60 yds.)

    A. Topaz
    B. Cobalt
    C. Midnight Blue
    D. Butterscotch
    E. Daisy

Note: You may see the line of joining where dark squares are joined to light squares. If this bothers you, try to substitute colors that are less contrasting.

NEEDLES: Double-pointed #3. *Note:* Directions are written for 4-needle socks. The stitches are divided evenly onto three needles and the fourth needle is used for working. To convert instructions to 5-needle socks, just divide instep sts evenly onto two needles instead of one.

GAUGE: 6 sts and 8 rnds = 1 inch (worked over stockinette stitch).

SIZES

    Child Large
    Adult Small and Medium
    Adult Large

Leg length and foot length are easily adjusted. To lengthen leg, add more rounds of squares. To lengthen foot, add more rounds before toe shaping.

(For information on converting measurements and needle sizes to metric equivalents, see page 33.)

PATTERNS

Stockinette Stitch: Knit every round.

K2, P2 Ribbing

Entrelac (explained below)

A NOTE ABOUT KNITTING BACKWARD, OR FROM LEFT TO RIGHT

Regular knitting involves working the stitches from the left needle onto the right needle. Knitting backward involves working the stitches from the right needle onto the left needle. The main advantage to this technique is that you do not need to turn your work in order to work a purl row. Stockinette stitch can be produced by working back and forth on straight needles with the right side facing at all times. This is a useful technique to use when working short rows where constant turning slows down the work. It is almost imperative to use when working entrelac, a knitting method that involves knitting bias squares one at a time.

Begin by practicing on a small swatch of about twenty stitches, working a foundation of a few rows in the traditional method of stockinette stitch. In order to learn how to create a purl stitch on the right side, it is helpful to study how the stitch is created on the wrong side in the traditional way. With a purl row facing you, purl a stitch, stopping halfway through the process. Turn your work to the right side and study what the stitch looks like—where the yarn is going, where it is coming from, and what the loops look like. Turn your work back to the wrong side and complete the stitch. Do this many times. Then try the backward method from the instructions that follow.

How to Knit Backward: All the stitches will be on your right-hand needle, the right side of the work will be facing you, and the yarn will be controlled by your right hand. Insert the left-hand needle through the back of the first stitch on the right needle. Wrap the yarn over the left needle and draw it through the stitch, sliding the right needle out of the old stitch. Remember that the stitches are being removed from the right needle and put on the left needle.

This method might seem a bit awkward at first, and you might even forget how to do it the next day. After a bit of practice, it will become second nature and part of your standard repertoire. These Entrelac Ski Socks are different and fun to knit, and will hone your backward-knitting skills to perfection.

RIBBING: With COLOR A, cast on very loosely 56–60–64 sts. Join. This is where all rnds begin and end. Work in K2, P2 ribbing for 3.5–4–4.5 inches, decreasing 8–6–4 sts evenly spaced on last rnd. (48–54–60 sts.) Adjust sts to have 12–18–18 on needle #1, 18 on needle #2, and 18–18–24 on needle #3.

ENTRELAC TECHNIQUE: You are now ready to begin the entrelac portion of the sock leg. The first part of this is to establish a series of base triangles from which the squares will be formed. When a row is to be worked backward, the abbreviation WB will be used.

Color Sequence: E, B, A, D, C. Work these five colors in sequence for each set of squares or triangles, then repeat the sequence again from the beginning.

Base Triangles: Use first color from sequence (COLOR E).

Row 1: K2.
Row 2. (WB) Slip 1, K1.
Row 3: Slip 1, K2.
Row 4: (WB) Slip 1, K2.
Row 5 Slip 1, K3.
Row 6: (WB) Slip 1, K3.
Row 7: Slip 1, K4.
Row 8: (WB) Slip 1, K4.
Row 9: Slip 1, K5.

These nine rows make one base triangle. Repeat them 7–8–9 more times for a total of 8–9–10 base triangles. On the last triangle only, work one additional row of: (WB) Slip 1, K5. This puts the yarn in the correct position to begin the next step.

Right-Slanting Square: Use second color from sequence (COLOR B). Using the right needle, pick up 5 loops through the backs of the stitches on the slip stitched edge of the triangle. Do not use the working yarn to pick up and knit the stitches; just lift up the loops and put them on the needle. The right edge of this square will be attached to the left edge of the triangle with every K2 together.

Row 1: (WB) K5, then knit the first live stitch from the corner of the triangle for a total of 6 sts.
Row 2: Slip 1, K5.
Row 3: (WB) Slip 1, K4, K2 together.
Rows 4–11: repeat rows 2 and 3 four more times.
These 11 rows complete the square. Make 7–8–9 more squares, for a total of 8–9–10 squares. On the last square only, work one additional row of: Slip 1, K5. This puts the yarn in the correct position for the next step.

Left-Slanting Square: Use third color from sequence (COLOR A). With the left needle, pick up 5 loops through the fronts of the stitches on the slip stitch edge of the last square worked. Do not use the working yarn; just lift up the loops onto the needle. The left edge of this square is being attached to the right edge of the adjacent square with every SSK.

Row 1: K5, K1 live stitch from the adjacent square for a total of 6 sts.
Row 2: (WB) Slip 1, K5.
Row 3: Slip 1, K4, SSK.
Row 4–11: repeat rows 2 and 3 four more times.
These 11 rows complete the square. Make 7–8–9 more squares, for a total of 8–9–10 squares. On the last row of the last square only, work one additional row of: (WB) Slip 1, K5. This puts the yarn in the correct position for the next step.

Repeat right-slanting squares and left-slanting squares in color sequence until you have a total of 7–9–11 sets of squares, the last set being composed of right-slanting squares, and having worked the one additional row to position yarn.

Finishing Triangles: Use COLOR E. With the left needle, pick up 5 loops through the fronts of the stitches on the slip stitch edge of the square. Do not use the working yarn; just lift up the loops onto the needle.

Row 1: K5, K 1 live stitch from the corner of the adjacent square for a total of 6 sts.
Row 2: (WB) Slip 1, K1.
Row 3: Slip 1, SSK.
Row 4: (WB) Slip 1, K2.
Row 5: Slip 1, K1, SSK.
Row 6: (WB) Slip 1, K3.
Row 7: Slip 1 K2, SSK.
Row 8: (WB) Slip 1, K4.
Row 9: Slip 1, K3, SSK.
Row 10: (WB) Slip 1, K5.
Row 11: Slip 1, K4, SSK.

These 11 rows complete the finishing triangles. You should now be in a vertical line where the rnd was joined at the ribbing.

BOTTOM OF LEG: Knit next rnd with COLOR E, increasing 0–2–4 sts evenly spaced. (48–56–64 sts.)

Next rnd: (WB) Slip 1 st, K 11–13–15 sts. Place these 12–14–16 sts plus another 12–14–16 sts from the other side of the join on a needle for the heel. Place other sts on a holder or needle for instep sts.

HEEL: (Reinforcing thread may be added if desired). Using COLOR B and, working back and forth, repeat the following two rows for a total of 20–24–28 rows, ending with a completed row 2.

Row 1: *Slip 1 st purlwise, K1*, repeat between *s.

Row 2: Slip 1 st purlwise, purl to end of row.

Turn Heel. Row 1: K 12–14–16 sts, K2, slip 1, K1, PSSO, K1. Turn work.

Row 2: Slip 1, P5, P2 together, P1. Turn work.

Row 3: Slip 1, knit to within 1 st of gap, slip 1, K1, PSSO, K1. Turn work.

Row 4: Slip 1, purl to within 1 st of gap, P2 together, P1. Turn work.

Repeat rows 3 and 4 until all sts are used up on both sides. (14–16–18 sts remaining)

Knit to middle of right-side row. (If reinforcing thread was used, break off here.) Break off Color B.

GUSSET AND FOOT: Attach COLOR A. With a new needle, knit the last half of the heel sts, with the same needle pick up and knit 10–12–14 sts down left side of heel, with a new needle work the instep stitches, with a new needle pick up and knit 10–12–14 sts up right side of heel, with the same needle, knit the remaining half of heel sts. (Needle #1 will have half of the heel sts plus the picked up sts from the side of the heel, needle #2 will have the instep sts, and needle #3 will have the picked up sts from the other side of the heel plus the last half of the heel sts.)

Rnd. 1 (decrease rnd). Needle #1: K 3 sts, K2 together, K1. Needle #2: K across all instep stitches. Needle #3: K1, SSK, K to end of needle.

Rnd. 2: Knit

Repeat these 2 rnds until 48–56–64 sts remain. Continue working even until 1–1.5–1.75 inches less than desired length for foot.

Work 4 rnds in COLOR D.

TOE SHAPING: Use COLOR B. (If reinforcing thread is desired, use for toe shaping too.)

Rnd. 1 (decrease rnd). Needle #1: K to last 3 sts, K2 together, K1. Needle #2: K1, SSK, work to last 3 sts, K2 together, K1. Needle #3: K1, SSK, work to end of needle.

Rnd. 2: Knit.

Repeat these two rnds until 24–28–32 sts remain.

Now work the decrease rnd only until 8 sts remain (2 sts each on needles #1 and #3, 4 sts on needle #2).

Break yarn. Weave sts together.

AMISH STAR MITTENS

The design for these mittens was inspired by the beautiful Amish quilts that use bright colors against a black background. This is the perfect project to use up odds and ends of yarn. (Pictured on page 23.)

YARN: Harrisville Shetland Style (50 gm/1.75 oz skeins), 1 skein of each color, or exact amounts listed below.

30 grams of Black (Main Color)
About 25 yards of each of the following colors:
A. Seagreen
B. Sea Mist
C. Chianti
D. Peony
E. Cobalt
F. Bermuda
G. Violet
H. Periwinkle
I. Peacock
J. Aqua Blue
K. Mulberry Tweed
L. Aster

NEEDLES: #2 and #3 double-pointed (sets of 5 needles). *Note:* Directions are written for 5 double-pointed needles. Stitches are divided onto 4 needles, and the fifth needle is used for working them. Stitches for the palm are on needles #1 and #2, and stitches for the back are on needles #3 and #4. Most American double-pointed needles come in packages of 4. Therefore, you may have to purchase two packages.

GAUGE: 27 sts and 31 rnds = 4 inches (worked over pattern on #3 needles).

FINISHED SIZE: Adult Medium.
Cuff length = 3.5 inches.
Length of mitten from top of cuff = 7 inches.
Circumference = 9 inches.

(For information on converting measurements and needle sizes to metric equivalents, see page 33.)

PATTERN. Stockinette Stitch: Knit every round.

LEFT MITTEN

CUFF: With MC and #2 needles, cast on 62 sts. Distribute sts onto 4 needles as follows:

Needle #1	15 sts
Needle #2	16 sts
Needle #3	15 sts
Needle #4	16 sts

Join rnd. All rnds begin and end between needle #4 and needle #1.

Purl 2 rnds, then K1 rnd.

Now work the following 4 rnds in each of the following colors: A, B, MC, C, D, MC, E, F, MC, K, L, MC.

Rnd. 1: Knit
Rnd. 2 and 3: Purl
Rnd. 4: Knit

HAND: Change to #3 needles and CHART A, working the 31 sts for palm on needles #1 and #2, and the 31 sts for back on needles #3 and #4. Work through rnd 18.

Thumb Opening: On rnd 19, work across the 15 sts of needle #1, work first 2 sts of needle #2, slip the next 12 sts onto a thread, cast on 12 sts in alternating colors, work last 2 sts of needle #2, work all sts of needles #3 and #4.

Continue working even through rnd 45.

TOP DECREASING (Rnds 45–55). Work decreases as follows:
Needle #1: K1, K2 together, work remaining sts.
Needle #2: Work to 3 sts before end, SSK, K1.
Needle #3: same as #1.
Needle #4: same as #2.

TOP FINISHING: Slip the 11 sts from needles #1 and #2 onto a safety pin, repeat for needles #3 and #4. Turn mitten inside out. Put 11 sts onto a double-pointed needle, put the other 11 sts onto a needle. Join the two sides using the knitted seam method.

LEFT THUMB: With MC and #3 needles, pick up and knit 1 st at right corner just before the sts on the thread, knit the 12 sts from the thread (distribute 6 sts on needle #1 and 7 sts on needle #2), pick up and knit 1 st at the corner after the stitches on the thread, pick up and knit 12 sts at cast on edge (distribute 6 sts on needle #3 and 7 sts on needle #4). All rnds begin and end between needle #4 and needle #1.

Work CHART B, working top decreasing and finishing same as mitten.

RIGHT MITTEN: Work same as left mitten, but working thumb opening rnd as follows: (Rnd. 19) Work 2 sts from needle #1, slip next 12 sts onto a thread, cast on 12 sts in alternating colors, work all remaining sts to end of rnd.

Work CHART C.

FINISHING: Steam lightly, stretching mitten gently lengthwise if needed.

CHART A: HAND

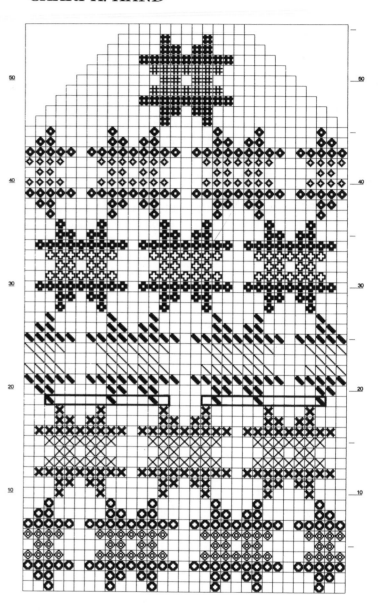

CHART B:
LEFT
THUMB

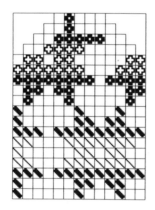

KEY FOR CHARTS

◘	A. Sea Green
◈	B. Sea Mist
✖	C. Chianti
⊠	D. Peony
◣	E. Coblt
◺	F. Bermuda
✜	G. Violet
⊡	H. Periwinkle
◆	I. Peacock
◇	J. Aquamarine
▦	K. Mulberry Tweed
⊞	L. Aster
☐	MC. main color—Black

CHART C:
RIGHT
THUMB

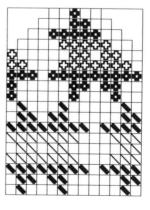